Fur babies

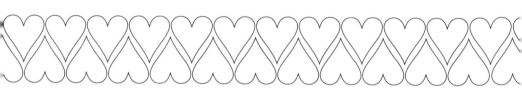

QUADRILLE

Fur Babies

WHY WE LOVE CATS

Liz Jones
and others

Why I am writing this book

Confessions of a cat woman

Fellow travellers

WHY I AM WRITING THIS BOOK

There are always awful animal-cruelty stories in the papers, but one that sent shivers down my spine for weeks afterwards was the story of an abandoned greyhound who was picked up by the police, placed in the pound at the station (awful, cold bunkers at the best of times), and then forgotten about. He was found weeks later having starved slowly to death. Then there was the bear in India who was kept at a zoo in a concrete cavern, with no company, nothing to play with. The only thing he could do all day was peer through a tiny hole in the wall at the outside world.

I am actually writing this in a wooden cabin in a forest in Newfoundland, where I am patiently awaiting the start of the annual 'hunt' (and I use that word lightly; locals call it a harvest, I call it a slaughter) of grey seal pups. Despite the fact that in the winter of 2006/7 the seals have suffered a terrible catastrophe because of global warming – the ice is not thick enough for them to give birth on, and so the pups, some 260,000 of them in the southern part of the Gulf of St Lawrence, simply drowned – the hunt is still due to take place.

Up to 300,000 pups will be hit over the head with a hakapik (a lovely instrument that is part club, part hook), and often skinned while still conscious. Many injured pups manage to crawl into the water, where they drown, but these pups, called in the business 'struck and lost', aren't included in the Canadian government's quota.

The saddest sight of all is that of the mother seals, who take to the water in fear when the hunt begins, returning to try to find their pups. You see them going through the pile of steaming carcasses, and the noise they make at this time is pitiful, and not easily forgotten.

So I don't understand people who say that animals don't have souls, that they can't feel pain or stress or love, and that they don't know exactly what we are thinking and feeling. My cats know that I love them, and I know they love me back (although that is not a prerequisite; loving me is totally *their choice*). When I get home late at night, and open the door to find Squeaky frantically scratching the mat and grunting, I can feel how desperately she wants to get across to me that she is glad to see me, wants to know where I have been and whether or not I have missed her, too. In all the thirteen years I have known her, she has never once missed our little greeting-on-the-mat ritual.

I rub her briskly on her ample rump, and she follows me down to the kitchen, 'Wah wahing' all the way, trying to tell me about her day and how annoyed she is I haven't been around. It's a real dialogue, me asking her if she is okay or what she wants for supper, her letting me know with a series of chirrups or squeaks or head butts. I have never been as close to anyone as I am to Squeaky. I don't think of her as a pet, more as a best friend.

Squeaks was not, strictly speaking, a rescue cat. I don't think she has ever lived in a cage, apart from an overnight stay at the vet's when I moved house last year (she attacked all the nurses and did great big poos on the blankets in protest). She just turned up in my sitting room one day, a tiny black kitten (well, not that tiny; she has always been very fond of food) and refused point blank to leave.

But two of my cats are rescues: Susie was one of a feral litter born on a pavement on the Isle of Dogs (she has blanked her poor beginnings from her mind, and is now very much a spoilt princess), and Sweetie had been abused as a kitten by her previous owners, who liked to strike her about the head. These little tabbies have The Celia Hammond Animal Trust (CHAT) in Canning Town, a particularly feral part of East London, as their *alma mater*, and it is because the tireless, hardworking Celia earmarked both of them just for me (she thought them specially difficult and especially cute) that I decided to compile a book to be sold to help the work she does.

Celia is almost unique in this country in that she rehabilitates feral cats; many other animal charities deem them too difficult to catch in the first place, and far too difficult to rehome. Having seen Celia, a *Vogue* model in the Sixties, lying on her stomach in a freezing cold factory in Docklands for hours while she waits for a cat to enter her humane trap, I know she never labels an animal a lost cause. Part of the money from the sale of this book will be used to help set up a sanctuary for very old feral cats who don't want to be 'normal' but need somewhere safe, where they can climb trees or just sit under them, where they have a warm place to sleep at night, and access to medication and help.

You can read more about the wonderful work Celia does on pages 54 to 59, but I hope you will also enjoy discovering why so many people have fallen under the spell of what I think I quite aptly call Fur Babies. These creatures are small, they are playful, they have huge personalities and they will, if you are nice enough to them, love you with a fierceness and a protectiveness that has to be felt to be believed.

Confessions of a cat woman

FEBRUARY 2007

Meet the most famous, and certainly best loved, cats in the world: Snoopy, the original cat; Squeaky, the fattest cat; Susie, the most contrary and spoilt cat; Sweetie (full name Sweetheart Biscuit Jones-Dhaliwal), the sweetest cat; and Leo, the occasional cat. Fur babies, all (and far, far more endearing than human babies, obviously).

What do I love about cats?

I love the fact they will choose a special place to sleep, and won't be budged from it for weeks (my Eames office chair, say), and then suddenly they have abandoned that place in favour of somewhere else (the spare bed). I love the way they lie in doorways, keeping their options open and allowing them to snoop in two rooms at once (cats are nothing if not nosey). I love the way they like to show off: leaping in one bound onto the garden wall or catching a toy in mid air. I love the way they will scratch your favourite sofa, and turn to look at you while they are doing it, as if to say, 'Look, Mummy!' (It is embarrassing to admit, but my husband and I call each other Mummy and Daddy while in the presence of our pussies.) I love the way cats always seem know what you are thinking. If I am watching telly but thinking about giving Squeaky her lunch, she will suddenly be all alert, and start squeaking.

I love the way they will sit, get this look on their faces, and then shoot a hind leg up in the air (cats are nothing if not designed to do yoga) as they get busy with a thorough wash (not Squeaky, who can only be bothered to attend to her face). I love the way they stretch, and yawn, and sleep on their backs, exposing their soft tummies. I love the way they sit all neat like teapots. I love the way they chirrup when they enter a room to make sure you know they are there. I love the fact all my female cats, even Susie, who is of supermodel proportions, have a little furry bag that swings beneath them as they walk.

Snoopy

Snoopy was my first cat. I got him as a kitten fourteen years ago. His mother, a black and white cat called Domino, had chosen my friend Simon's bedroom in which to deliver a litter of kittens, and Snoopy, because he was a boy, was the last to be homed. I picked him up in my ancient Beetle, putting him in a cardboard carrier, and drove him home. He cried all the way from the Elephant and Castle in South London to my flat in Old Street, and eventually chewed his way out of the box and set about exploring the car. When I got him home, he immediately used the litter tray (he is such a good little boy; even when he has been coming round from anaesthetic after one of his many operations, he has always dragged himself to his litter tray), and then slept soundly on my pillows for almost twenty-four hours.

Snoopy is a shy little cat, and hates too much attention or fuss. But over the years he has become more confident (thanks largely to my husband, who started kissing him on his forehead, something he now loves and actively seeks out). Recently he has started climbing onto me in the middle of the night, giving me a quick head butt, reaching forward for his forehead kiss, and then settling down to sleep peacefully, curled tightly like a catherine wheel on my tummy.

Snoopy is rescued by the fire brigade

The reason I got a cat in the first place was because I had just split up with my boyfriend (I use the term lightly) Trevor. I thought a cat would prove far better company than a monosyllabic nightmare who refused to acknowledge that we were going out, despite the fact he had lived in my flat for three years, and I was proved right. Snoopy became someone I rushed home to at night, whom I lovingly prepared supper for rather than haring round M&S in my lunch hour for a ready meal, who was funny (he loved to pull himself along the bottom of my sofa upside down) and sweet and affectionate. He also loved to explore and put his nose into things, hence his name.

When Trevor finally decided to move his stuff out and packed all his things in boxes (hundreds and hundreds of hip-hop CDs), Snoopy had a fine time exploring all the newly empty shelves. But then he suddenly became immobile and started to cry (Snoopy, not Trevor, whom I was certain was glad to be shot of me; he soon moved in with a diminutive woman with a head wrap and a 'real' child), and I realised he had got his head stuck through a hole in one of the shelves. No matter how hard I tried, I could not pull him out. And so, naturally, I dialled 999.

'What emergency service are you calling for?' asked the kind lady on the switchboard. I explained the situation and she suggested the fire brigade. Within five minutes, an enormous red engine had pulled up outside my flat, and six huge men were in my front room pondering the situation. I suggested they saw through the shelves, but one of them thought we should try coating Snoopy's neck with butter and gently pulling him backwards. It worked, although, obviously, being a vegan, we had to use olive oil spread!

The exploding face and other escapades

Snoopy has got into many scrapes over the years. About a year after that olive oil spread episode, he went missing for exactly two weeks (I guess he must have gone on a package holiday). I was frantic. I put up notices on all the lampposts in my street, phoned the local vet's, knocked door to door, but no luck. Then, on a Friday night, having lost all hope of ever seeing his little tabby face and his white bib and four immaculate white socks again, I got home to find him sitting in the kitchen, covered in grey grime. I scooped him up in my arms, and discovered he was as light as a feather; he'd lost almost all his body weight.

I took him straight to the vet, who gave him an injection to help boost his immune system, announced he was lucky to be alive, and told me to allow him only very small meals, several times a day, for a couple of weeks. Snoopy has never really been his former self since (you can always feel the notches in his spine, and he hasn't developed the trademark baggy tummy of my other cats, but maybe that is because he is a boy). Still, thankfully, he has never gone missing again.

But I almost lost him once more a couple of years ago, when he suddenly got much thinner, and just sat in a corner, doing his very best teapot impression. My husband, during one of his lingering kisses (not with me, with the cat), noticed Snoopy smelt a bit odd, but we didn't know why. Then, one morning, I spotted splashes of blood and yellow pus (or is that 'puss'?) on the walls of the kitchen, and saw to my horror that Snoopy's face had exploded.

The vet explained that Snoopy must have been fighting, and because of his weak state was unable to defend himself properly (but the brave little cat had been bitten on his face and not his bottom, which meant he was involved in a stand-off and not beating a hasty retreat, and had developed abscesses, which had burst). The pain he was in (he had another abscess on a front paw, which he must have held up to protect himself) just does not bear thinking about. I will always feel such a terrible mummy for not having noticed the problem much earlier.

But the wounds were a symptom of something much more serious. What on earth was making him so weak and defenceless? Numerous tests were run; they showed nothing. Eventually, the vet decided to open him up. We went to visit Snoopy that night in the clinic (he was sitting in a little cage on his special blanket), and to all intents and purposes we said goodbye to him.

I remember it was a hot summer, and my husband stood in the garden later that night, drinking gin and tonic (something he would never normally do) and smoking a cigarette, saying he was glad we didn't have children because he didn't think he could bear to feel so much despair ever again. (I don't know why people always say that the love a parent feels for a child is so much deeper than the love you feel for a pet. Do parents really love their children so much? I would never shout at my pussies, or slap them on their legs, or tell them to move out when they reach eighteen, or drag them round supermarkets. I feel the need to point out here the disparity in status afforded to mummies of human babies and mummies of fur ones. When I took custodyship of Snoopy, I should have been entitled to kitty leave, surely?)

Anyway, the next day, the vet rang to say that Snoopy was coming round, and that they had been able to diagnose pancreatitis (which means Snoopy was unable to digest food, particularly fat, properly), which is treatable. He now takes steroids every day, and has to eat a low-fat diet, but on the whole he is as right as rain. And he no longer fights, preferring to stay in at night on his mummy's tummy.

Squeaky

I think Squeaky and I were meant to be together. She is my soul mate. I love her more than anyone in the world (although, of course, my cats know that I love them all equally). She is black and very round, with a round face and big, round orange eyes. I think she must be part Burmese because her fur is very soft and dense, like velvet, or that found on a mole. I didn't find Squeaky, she found me. I got home from work one evening, about two years after Snoopy moved in, and there was a very round black kitten motoring around my sitting room. I assumed she belonged to someone and so I put her in the garden and locked the cat flap. She wouldn't budge, and proceeded to batter the flap until I let her back in. We haven't been separated since.

Apart from the greetings-on-the-mat ritual I mentioned at the beginning of this book, Squeaky and I have gotten into a routine that we are both comfortable with, and would miss dearly. At bedtime, as soon as she hears my electric toothbrush, she will waddle upstairs and get onto the bed, taking up as much room as possible. She likes to lie slap bang in the middle, on the pillows, just to annoy my husband. In the morning, as soon as she knows I am awake, she will sit up and gaze, all bright eyed and bushy tailed, into my face. She is always so cheerful first thing that she never fails to make me smile, even when she decides to lick my face with her rough little pink tongue, sit on my hair and finally knead my scalp with her front paws.

Watching TV, she will always sit next to me, the remote control between her paws or as a pillow (she hates not to have jurisdiction over it). When I am working at my desk, she loves to sit right by the keyboard, and if I ignore her for too long she reminds me she is there by giving me a swipe. She is the *grande dame* of my four cats, and the others make sure they give her a wide berth. She keeps them under control, and I love her so much that just thinking about her makes me want to cry.

Winner of the best-tail competition Squeaky would never go missing because she hates the garden, hates climbing up onto things, and only ever explored next door when a storm blew the fence over. Her favourite pastimes are sleeping, eating, being in charge of the remote control, and licking me. She has been known to lash out at my husband, particularly when he first moved in. She was jealous that somebody else was now sleeping with me, and did her best to discourage him. To my husband's credit, he soon learned to sleep like a starfish, a cat nestled in any one of the various angles, and not to move, or roll over. He also quickly became used to a banshee-like shriek of 'Mind Squeaky!!' if ever he looked poised to sit on her (Squeaky, it has to be said, is not exactly quick off the mark).

She is the most talkative of my cats. If you ask her something, anything ('Hello, Squeaky, how are you, my darling?'), she will reply with a 'Hmmm'. My husband always puts her on the phone when I am away and she chirrups down the line to me, pleased to hear my voice. She has been on a diet for most of her life, but refuses to lose a gram. We tried her on those awful diet cat-biscuits but she just sucks them and spits them out around her bowl. She is such a lazy cat. She can only be bothered to waddle to the cat litter in the garden before high-tailing it back into the house (her tail is always straight up, like a mast. On one of his less frantic days my husband phoned me at work to say he was holding a competition to see which cat had the best tail; Squeaky won. Susie's tail is too thin, Snoopy's too fluffy and Sweetie's is too big for her – in fact Sweetie more closely resembles a squirrel than a cat).

Squeaky isn't close to any of the other cats, preferring to share my chair with me while I work, and to sleep with me. My husband, who is home more than I am, says that Squeaky always knows ahead of time when I am about to open the front door. When I am abroad she knows the day I am due to fly home, starts becoming agitated that morning, and will waddle to sit on the mat, waiting for me, sometimes for hours on end. Squeaky knows when I am upset, or ill, and sometimes I can feel her frustration at not being able to communicate with me more directly, or reach out to me when I need help in some practical way.

Squeaky wears the cat flap as a skirt I once asked a cat psychiatrist to talk to Squeaky because I was so worried about her weight. She was finding it impossible to jump up onto the kitchen table (there is no work surface – bread boards included – that goes unsat upon by my kitties' bottoms) without a chair being strategically placed first. Now, a great deal of scrabbling goes on before she can get onto the bed; her little wide-eyed face often appears on the brink of the duvet, as if she has reached the summit of Everest, before she disappears back down again with a thud. The moment I realised I had to do something drastic was when she appeared, deeply embarrassed, in the kitchen with the cat flap stuck around her ample midriff, like a skirt or a tutu. I had to pull it off her while trying not to laugh (cats hate it if you laugh at them), and she now refuses point blank to go through the flap, and instead will sit and wait patiently until I open the door for her.

My husband had been insisting that Squeaky was deeply unhappy and neurotic ('Like his mummy'), and the cat psychiatrist agreed with him. 'Squeaky needs to learn how to be a cat again,' she said firmly. 'She spends all day just waiting to see you, and she should be outside hunting and doing what cats do. You need to make sure she exercises every day. You need to play with her, dangle a toy just in front of her face [Squeaky hates things being dangled in front of her face; she just lies on her back and does the occasional swipe]. She needs to separate from you.'

Well, I don't think Squeaky wants to be a cat. She is the most sensual, lazy, comfort-loving creature I know. She loves being stroked under her chin, and having her rump rubbed, and leaning against me. She loves organic prawns from M&S. She loves radiators. She loves telly. She loves my pillows. She loves cheese. She loves chocolate. She loves rubbing her head against a watch.

I don't think she has ever been out at night; I go to sleep and she is there and when I wake up she is there still, usually in exactly the same position. She snores, too, but she has never, in all our years together, brought me anything but joy, something I cannot say for my husband. I bought Squeaky a clockwork mouse recently, which she loves because it makes a great pillow. I think, I hope, that she is happy.

Susie

I don't know why we decided to get another cat. Perhaps we believed having a kitten to look after would cement our relationship, but I think not. I have seen so many couples do that very thing with babies and it never works out. I simply believed that I could offer a loving home to someone who didn't have one, and so I called the wonderful organisation run by Celia Hammond.

First, though, we had to be vetted as potential parents, and Celia turned up one evening to inspect our house. I was worried that if she spotted Squeaky I would lose custody of her, but we got a clean bill of health, and a few days later we drove to the clinic in Canning Town to make our selection. Celia had been able to tell by the way I opened the front door (only a crack, in case a puss made a frantic bid for freedom; they are not allowed out of the front of the house as it leads onto the road) and by the way I spoke about my two cats and their likes and dislikes that I was almost as obsessed with felines as she is, and so she asked if we would like to adopt a feral cat. A feral is a cat that has grown up wild, and is therefore afraid of humans and difficult to domesticate.

Unlike many animal charities which deem ferals to be nothing more than vermin, Celia manages to rescue and rehabilitate them. Adult ferals, perhaps rescued from living in a car park or on a building site, are trapped and neutered, and then set free in a more hospitable environment (on a cat-friendly farm, say). Kitten ferals are usually homed, but they require enormous amounts of patience and vigilance.

Celia showed us a family of feral kittens who had just been trapped on the Isle of Dogs (they had been born on a pavement; unfortunately, Celia had not been able to trap the mother). The six kittens were all wound up together in a stripey knot, and I took an immediate shine to two of the three tabbies. They were absolutely beautiful, with perfect markings, like mini leopards, and no white bits. Celia scooped them up (the kittens were so shocked and terrified they were all silent), and put them in our basket.

Living with a feral cat

Once home, we put them in the spare bedroom (the only room without a chimney; ferals are like Steve McQueen's character in *The Great Escape*, impossible to contain) and they immediately hid in the gaps between books on the bookshelf. We couldn't stroke them or even get near them. They were both very thin, and very wormy. Eventually, they made it to the sanctuary of a furry (not real fur, obviously) cat igloo and I remember watching as my husband, all fifteen stone of him, knelt before it, wiggling a tentative finger, which Susan, the feistier and livelier of the two, immediately pounced on with a ferocious hiss.

We soon noticed that the smaller of the two tabbies, Sesame, was not eating. I watched with horror as she walked along a desk and then simply dropped off the edge; she didn't land on her feet either but just fell, with an awful thud. I rang Celia and she told me to bring her straight back to the clinic. The vet (both she and Celia live in two rooms above the clinic) couldn't find out what was wrong, and agreed that eating only seemed to make her worse. Eventually, she was driven at speed up the motorway to a specialist who diagnosed that Sesame, like her other tabby sister (not Susie, thankfully), had a genetic abnormality that meant that some of her organs were back to front, and possibly missing. She died on the operating table.

I think the fact Susie lost her sister so young (she knew Sesame was ill because she kept grooming her) made her very mistrustful and wary. It took a year before I felt confident enough to let her out in the garden. It has taken five years for her to sit on the sofa with me to watch TV, and she will leap off, fur bristling, if I so much as sneeze, or change channels. Of all the cats she loves being stroked the most (she will head butt me with a dreamy look in her eyes to make me continue) but she refuses, point blank, to be picked up. She loves being tickled on top of her head, responding with a very good impression of Stan Laurel.

She is a very fussy eater; in this respect I think she takes after her mummy (i.e., me, not the mummy left behind on the Isle of Dogs). She has to be in the right mood, the bowl has to be placed in one of her favourite spots (all last summer it had to be on top of the garden wall), and the food has to be 'human'; Susan, despite her lowly beginnings, is far too beautiful and aristocatic [sic] to eat anything so mundane and smelly and common as cat food.

I wouldn't recommend adopting a feral if you have friends, or a life, or are in any way impatient. Susie hates it if a stranger comes to the house, and so we have just stopped inviting anyone round. She hates the postman, she hates the telephone, she hates the smoothie maker. But most of all (of which much more later) she hates our newest arrival, Sweetie, who insists on chasing Susie whenever she spots her, and has occasionally, using the element of surprise, managed to put her fat paws around Susie's elegant waist, filling her with absolute horror and disgust.

Susie goes AWOL I knew something was up because I was calling and calling Susie in the garden to come in for her tea, and she didn't drop silently and softly, as if by parachute, into the middle of the lawn. I stood on a flowerpot to look next door and spotted her on the fence gazing, with a determined and transfixed expression, into the distance. I told my husband that it was all rather weird; Susie could hear me, but she was deliberately ignoring me. That night, she woke me up for her supper, but in the morning she was nowhere in sight. It was a Saturday, and I had to go to the Cannes film festival, which I hated doing without first being sure that Susie was safe, but my husband assured me he would keep calling her.

When I returned on Monday he still hadn't seen her. I stood in the garden, calling and calling and whistling. All that week she still didn't appear, and I started to roam the streets at night with a torch, calling and then listening for her little high voice. I delivered about four hundred leaflets, with her picture and the offer of a hefty reward. Nothing. I began to think a fox might have eaten her, but when I rang Celia for advice she told me that foxes rarely eat cats; they are more likely to survive on rubbish scraps and insects. We were due to go to Mauritius for a week, but I cancelled it; I couldn't leave without knowing Susie was safe. I even contacted a psychic to see if she could tell me whether Susie was still alive and where to look, but all she said was she thought Susie had gone to the left. That was a fat lot of help.

Found at last! In the second week, on the Wednesday evening, I was on my own and so tearfully watched *Cold Mountain*, and then went and stood in the garden at about 11 p.m. to call Susie's name. I thought I heard a mew. I called again. There it was again. I thought it was her, but couldn't understand why, if she heard me, she didn't come. Then there was silence. I went to bed and when my husband came home

I told him I thought I had heard something. 'Well, if that was her she can come home if she wants to. I told you my theory. She wants to be free, to do her own thing. She isn't lost – in fact, I am sure Snoopy has seen her – but you have to face the fact she doesn't want to live with us any more. I told you she was behaving strangely that night. When you gave her supper you should have shut her in.'

Oh, of course, so Susie going missing was suddenly all my fault. And don't you just hate it when someone is brutal and honest and refuses to look on the bright side? The next night, I called and listened again, but there was nothing. On the Friday, we went out for dinner and as soon as we got home I went into the garden to call her. This time, I just knew it was her. I ran indoors. 'I can hear her, I can hear Susie!'

My husband came outside to join me and we listened. There it was. 'Ewww. Ewww.' We worked out, with much shushing, that it was coming from next door's garden. 'She must be in the Wendy house,' I hissed at him. The people next door were on holiday and so I clambered over the fence, armed with a Chanel torch, and crept over to the Wendy house. 'Can you see her? Can you see her?' my husband was saying. I opened the little door a crack, was hit by a terrible stench, shone the light inside and there, all alert and perky and cross, was my little girl. I shut the door. 'It's Susie, it's Susie!' I yelled. 'Get a bowl of water and a cat basket!'

Once inside (the stench was urine, which covered every mini chair and hideous doll and worn teddy), I held out the water bowl for my Susie, and she lapped frantically without taking her beady eyes off me. She was pleased to see me but she was very scared, and starving. I opened the cat basket, knowing I had only one chance to grab her, and I did. I don't know where she got the energy from as she wrestled and writhed, shredding my arms, but I held on and stuffed her inside.

As I handed her over the fence to my husband I could see from the moonlight bouncing off his face that he was crying. With no thought to me getting back over the thorny fence, he carried her away to put her in the spare bedroom with some water and food before returning to help me. When we both went to peer at her under the bed, I noticed she was covered in blood. 'Oh my God, she is injured!' I yelled, but my husband pointed out the blood was mine. I hadn't noticed in the excitement that my arms were covered with deep scratches.

I don't think Susie could have been in the Wendy house for two weeks because I am sure she would have died. And I would have heard her in the first week. I think she was on her way home and somehow, probably through the actions of some careless children, got shut in. But from the stench and her level of emaciation I am sure she had been in there for a week. Thank heavens I'd refused to give up calling her name. Because Susie knew when it was time to call for help. And I heard her.

Moving Susie

We moved house a year ago, from Hackney to Islington, and I have to admit what stressed me most about the whole thing was the prospect of moving Susie. I decided to keep her in for a week before the move date (cats are very good at picking up vibes), and then the day before the move I took them all to my local vet to remain under lock and key until we were safely in our new house. I hadn't picked up Susie since that night in the Wendy house, but as it turned out she was so shocked that I had both hands round her waist that she went along with it. I felt terrible putting Sweetie back in a cage too, when we had only had her for a year, and she gave me a look as if to say, 'But I've been good, I thought you loved me.'

When I went to pick them up (and Squeaky had been the naughtiest guest at the vet, biting everyone), I swear they all looked pleased to see me, but very put out. We kept them in for six weeks while I explored my options. I considered having some sort of lion cage built over the garden; then I considered an invisible radio force field that would emit a horrid noise if they went near it. In the end, I talked to them. I told them we had moved, that they should never leave all the gardens at the back of the house, and bless their souls they never have.

They love their new home. Squeaky is getting much more exercise going up and down the stairs, and has taken to lying in wait behind doors before pouncing on Sweetie. Sweetie loves watching the goldfish, and stealing their food. Snoopy is glad just to sit on the wall and survey his new kingdom. What with the meals-on-the-wall scenario, I was worried that Susie might never come into the house again, but about a week before Bonfire Night she decided, rightio, I am going to be a normal cat. She walked, tail up straight, into the kitchen, plonked herself down, stuck a hind leg in the air as if she were Darcey Bussell, and had a vigorous wash. She now spends every night indoors, on the 1920s elephant club chair in the sitting room (she pulls a face if you ever dare to sit in it). Once winter came, she became the most indoor of all the cats (I do recommend underfloor heating if you really want your cat to adore you), apart from Squeaky, of course.

Sweetie

Sweetie is a tomboy, always looking for mischief. She is very furry, with a tail that was at first too big for her. She has a crooked mouth that doesn't close properly, so you can always see a little pink tongue and a row of tiny white teeth. She is the gentlest, sweetest cat, who growls if you pick her up, and then attacks your ankles in revenge. She follows me all around the house. When I am working, I look down and there she is, at my feet.

She is a clumsy little cat (I have seen her stretch and tumble over the side of the bed more than once) and finds it very hard to climb onto the garden wall. She uses the branches of the wisteria as a sort of ladder, and then launches herself onto next door's lawn. She is always excited, galloping round the kitchen and then out the cat flap, and is constantly on the look out for Susie, whom she loves to chase (Susie is so gentle that even when she was twice her size, she would never turn round and clout Sweetie), and Snoopy, whom she has a bit of a crush on. They often touch noses and, when Sweetie wants to romp, he just sits there patiently, letting her play with his tail.

How Sweetie came to live with us

We got Sweetie by accident. I had spent Christmas helping clean the cages at Celia's clinic, and she kept telling me about a sweet little tabby who had just been brought in. Her family had been hitting her about the head so she might be a bit brain damaged; they'd also managed to chip a tooth. I told Celia that I would consult my husband, but that I didn't want to see the kitten, only a few months old, because I knew I would not be able to resist her. Then I went back to work, and Celia, never one to give up when faced with a challenge, phoned my husband direct to ask him what we had decided.

This happened to be at a terrible time for us. My husband's best friend was dying of cancer at the age of thirty-nine, and he had spent the last two years visiting her, going with her to hospital, running errands and just trying to be there for her. This was a very noble thing for him to do but, because he was so angry that she was dying, he had started to take everything out on me. And so I thought the last thing we needed was another cat. But on his way home from seeing B he popped into Celia's clinic, and held this little kitten in the palm of his hand. She started growling and chewing ferociously on his thumb, and he fell in love with her. He phoned me at work and told me he had named her Sweetie, and that he was bringing her home. B died the next day.

The day she learned to purr

Of all our cats, Sweetie is the most pet-like. She is always hanging around, always up for a tickle. She loves being kissed, and if I put my face close to hers and kiss her on her button nose she licks me in my mouth (she prefers me to my husband; if he tries to do the same thing she bites him on his nose). She licks her lips for about an hour after eating, and loves to be fed bits of organic chicken by hand. She loves to sleep on our big bed, both paws covering her eyes. She loves to sit by the pond, watching the goldfish feeding; they hate her, and splash her deliberately. She loves to march, sticking her front paws straight out. She loves to sit and stare into the middle distance. She loves dental floss, although it is very dangerous and must be disposed of safely. She is quite a common little cat, and loves junk food, namely Whiskas, which my husband occasionally sneaks her when I am not around, like an indulgent and misguided parent taking a child to McDonalds.

She rarely miaows, but I have learned from Snoopy and Squeaky that cats become more talkative as they get older. Still, if you fail to notice her come into a room she will let you know with a sound that is a cross between a yawn and a yap. It puzzled us that she never purred (perhaps the abuse she suffered as a baby was not forgotten), but one day recently, while I was in New York working, my husband called me, sounding all excited. 'Listen,' he said. And he put the phone next to Sweetie. I couldn't hear a thing. 'What?' 'She is purring!!' 'What did you do to her to make her do that?' 'I have been massaging her paw pads,' he said proudly.

Leo

It beggars belief how anyone can be mean to something so small and powerless as a cat, but there we go. Walk between the rows of cages at Celia's clinic in Canning Town, and she will recount heartbreaking story after heartbreaking story. Take a little old lady called Missy, who was living in the garden of some pensioners who wouldn't let her in because she had fleas. Or Scruff, who lived in a cardboard box in the corner of a car park (her owners had moved and left her behind) and she was being kicked around like a football by a gang of feral girls. Or Oliver, who is FIV positive. Or Martha, who had her kittens on a freezing doorstep; most of them died.

I can't understand people who see a stray and do not help it. Would you like to sleep outside, with nothing to eat? Cats, more than any other animal, love their creature comforts, and will always seek out a patch of sunlight to bask in or a feather pillow on which to rest their heads.

Not long after we moved into our new house, a scruffy black cat kept appearing on the windowsill, eating the cats' biscuits. I supposed he must belong to someone, and didn't think much of it. Then, on a really cold day, he came into the kitchen, started to enjoy the underfloor heating, and I noticed he had a big hole in the middle of his forehead. I managed to pick him up (he was very friendly) and took him to my vet.

Our honorary pet It turned out he was only nine months to a year old, was covered in bite wounds that had become abscesses, crawling with fleas, and had not been microchipped or neutered. We thought he must be a stray, so shocking was his condition, and I left him overnight to be neutered, vaccinated, chipped and given painkillers and antibiotics (although I am very holistic when it comes to my own health, when it comes to that of my cats every scientific advancement known to mankind is brought to bear). When I picked him up the next day, he seemed quite pleased to see me, and was confined to barracks for a few days, in my husband's office.

After about a week, I let him out, complete with collar and nametag. That afternoon, I got a phone call. 'Why have you put a collar on my cat?' said a very irate woman. When I pointed out the condition of the cat, and asked why he had not been neutered, she replied, 'I just hadn't got around to it.' And so it turns out I spent £400 on someone else's cat. But it was worth it. When he pops by to see us he looks like a different boy, all sleek and beautiful, his ear still torn but his wounds all healed. He is a sort of honorary pet, and he knows that if things get bad at home he always has us to fall back on.

Confessions of a cat woman

APRIL 2007

Why fur babies are better than human ones, why cat mummies are far better than smug, self-centred, always moaning human mummies, and why – just because I didn't squeeze Susie or Sweetie out between my thighs – I don't love them any less.

Are fur babies really substitutes for bald human ones?

Well, okay, I admit it. I am a mad old cat lady. I don't have children. There is no prospect or possibility that I will ever have children, as my last childbearing years were cruelly stolen from me by my non-lovemaking, change-his mind-about-adoption husband, who is now my ex-husband, and who in the hotly contested divorce proceedings did not try to get custody of the cats, not even Sweetie, which just goes to show how cold and cruel and heartless most men are.

But, if I am honest, I have never, ever dreamed of becoming a mum, not properly; I might give a second glance to a particularly dark-eyed, hair-bobbed tot, but I am much more inclined to coo and bend down to chuck under the chin of a sturdy ginger tom at the side of the road, or a wiry terrier sat in a gastro pub. I have been known to complain about children vociferously on planes (their noise, their running around, their endless germs); who on earth would take a newborn baby to Dar-es-Salaam, for goodness' sake?

Why do nursing mums automatically get the bulkhead seat? Surely that's discrimination? Didn't mothers choose to have their children, and therefore shouldn't they pay for the privilege? And isn't having a child decidedly ungreen and bad for the environment? Think of all the nappy mountains, the footstep that will grow and grow and procreate? Why don't I get tax credits for being a cat lover?

As a child, I dreamed of owning a palomino pony. I didn't own a single doll or a pram; I had a Cindy, but the only outfit she possessed was a riding habit, the only accessory a bay horse. As an adolescent and throughout my twenties I was horse mad (although I have to say my horse, a crazy bay thoroughbred called Monty, wasn't mad about me and bit me whenever he thought I was going to steal his hay net and liked to walk me into a bed of nettles).

In my thirties, I treated any unfortunate man who made a stab at being my boyfriend like a giant pet, a practice that continued into my so-called marriage. With one baby already in the family (namely, my husband), there certainly wasn't room for a human one, and so all the love I had stored up in me was foisted on my cats, who increased in number along with my extreme sense of loneliness in the relationship.

Earth mothers and other monsters

Actually, the attitude of mothers towards a woman with cats makes my blood boil, and I immediately want to serve their boisterous offspring a sandwich that has been pre-licked by Snoopy, or sat on by Sweetie.

I know one particularly horrid earth mother with two children who got two cats 'for the children' (a stupid, misguided reason if ever I heard one), and then proceeded to confine the poor creatures to a cold kitchen without a soft surface or radiator hammock to be seen. She says she is 'worried about cat hair'; this is a woman whose house resembles a bomb site, with socks on the stairs, bottles in the bathroom that have never seen an antiseptic wipe, and furniture that a darn good scratching would probably improve.

I am positive that I get more pleasure, more unconditional love and sweet, Kodak moments from my cats than any mother does from her overindulged, overpraised children – who, after all, will mutate into sullen teenagers and then flee the nest, possibly occasionally visiting you in your state-run nursing home to ask where you keep your jewellery.

I truly believe that mothers (particularly middle-class earth types who still breast feed when their child is nearly three) have children as something to do with their otherwise empty lives; they need to be smug, to have something over on their husbands (who never wanted kids in the first place and would far prefer a spaniel), and to boss around and organise. I don't think parents who adopt are quite as bad, as long as they do it for at least some of the right reasons.

Loving cats is making them the centre of things

There was a brief window (nay, barely a front-door spyhole) a few years back when I did actually consider adopting a child from India with my now ex-husband, who is of Indian origin. Although perhaps uppermost in my mind should have been the facts that I was always working in an office and travelling, that my husband would never help and get cross and would probably leave us, the thought that kept coming unprompted into my head was, 'What if the cats don't like her? What if she is noisy and keeps squealing or trying to kick them? What if Susie decides to run away again?' And at that point I realised that I would never love another human the way I love my cats.

I can't imagine loving something more just because you squeezed it out between your thighs. I couldn't love Susie or Sweetie more if I had actually given birth to them, although I still wish they had some contact with their real fur mummies. Having cats, as opposed to children, isn't about me or my needs or a wild stab at status or acceptability or being normal. It is about them, giving them a lovely home, and pillows, and the best food, and protecting them and talking to them and making them feel important and the centre of things (cats hate it if you ignore them. I recently worked out why Squeaky, who likes to make her habitual 'puddle' shape on my desk, will often swipe me when she is next to my laptop; it is because I am caressing the keys and not her, and looking at the screen and not at her).

Cats are far better than men

I firmly believe that cats are not only better than children; they are far, far better than men, too. If there is a weird noise in the middle of the night, Sweetie will sit up straight, fur on end, her weird squirrelly tail twice its size, her eyes like saucers, and she will pad around the house with me, looking for monsters. Men, on the other hand, will remain fast asleep, impervious to the danger and emitting weird, cabbagey smells when my cats smell only of teddy-bear fur.

The wonderful Ingrid Newkirk, who co-founded People for the Ethical Treatment of Animals (PETA) and wrote the indispensable guide to having a happy cat at the back of this book, once told me that cats like to watch over their humans while they are sleeping because this is when we are at our most vulnerable. Our cats feel it is their duty to look after us, not the other way around, and I believe this is absolutely true. I know that Snoopy in particular looks out for me; he really does seem to beam out a special spirit or aura that transcends the fact he is made of fur and I'm not.

I know my cats are not thinking horrible thoughts about me, or wondering why I haven't got make-up on today, or aren't I getting perilously close to the menopause, or whether the nice lady down the road would serve up better suppers and perform fellatio more often. No, my cats are immensely loyal to me. I know that if they left me it would be because something awful had happened to them (a child closing the door of a Wendy house without checking inside first) and they couldn't get back.

No more whiffy yoga kit When I finally split up with my husband after four years of marriage, the first and in fact the only thing that flashed through my mind was, What about the pussy cats? Who would look after them when I had to travel for work? We were on a two-week holiday in Africa when he told me he had had another affair (his seventh), and it is shameful to admit but an enormous part of me was thinking, 'Hoorah! I can send him back home and he can relieve the sitter and look after the cats full time.' And when he begged me to let him stay for the rest of the holiday, I was thinking, 'No, you can't. I will enjoy it so much more if I know the cats are okay.'

I could understand him wanting to cheat on me and leave me (as anyone who has read my previous book, *Liz Jones's Diary*, the story of our six-year-long tumultuous and torturous relationship, will know I am not the most confident, self-assured person in the world), but when

I got back from holiday to find him gone, as well as all his awful sportswear, trainers and decidedly whiffy yoga kit, I could only wonder at the soul of a man who could close the door behind him, knowing that he would never again set eyes on the sweet, crooked little face of Sweetie, or the kind, wise, knowing face of Snoopy. How men leave their babies, fur or otherwise, I cannot begin to fathom.

And I have to say that having my four cats around me when I got back from Africa and found the house otherwise empty has been an enormous solace. They are taking it in turns to make sure I am never alone, not even when I am in the bath. Three of them are now sleeping with me, and they keep giving me concerned looks and winding between my ankles. They were unsettled when my husband left (I had sent him a firm text, telling him that he should be careful when emptying the chest of drawers of his hideous sportswear, as Sweetie has a thing about drawers), but I am sure they are happier that it is now just us.

My husband had the annoying habit of picking Sweetie up and cradling her in his arms like an infant, exposing her soft tummy, which she found very stressful and undignified. 'You are making her bitey and scratchy!' I would wail endlessly, feeling like some dreadful mum who refuses to kick out her boyfriend despite the fact he smacks her children and feeds them sweets.

My cats keep me sane They render impossible the sort of obsessive-compulsive lifestyle I would otherwise slip into. They have paws, which leave little sweaty marks. They go outside, which means they bring mud, and leaves, and dirt into the house. They (and although I say 'they', I think the culprit is, in reality, Sweetie) have shredded my brand new toffee-coloured Jasper Morrison sofa. They cover my Conran bedlinen with hair. They smudge the cat flap. They eat smelly food (although not as smelly as cat food, tuna for humans is still slightly pungent). Sweetie in particular makes such a mess, because of her wonky mouth: food and biscuits are scattered around her bowl and I rarely see her washing, she is always far too busy. And because of them I have to buy cat litter (although the tray is in the garden, because I don't like them to use my flower beds).

My cats make me far less selfish and self-centred; their presence means I put someone else before myself. And although, as someone recently said to me, they are not 'designer' (she had expected my pussies to be expensive, with a pedigree and all that came with it), to me my cats are the most beautiful in the world. Much as Kate Moss wouldn't be as gorgeous had she royal blood, so Susie would not have quite the same cachet had she been hot-housed by some awful breeder. (She is the most spoilt being I have ever come across.) My cats couldn't possibly have been bought for mere money, like some piece of Louis Vuitton hand luggage. My cats came to me quite by chance. I think there was a higher being who was acting as matchmaker.

I cannot imagine life without my cats. How boring and sterile and empty would it be? When my husband announced he had moved out, I felt not a twinge of regret, not a smidgen of remorse. I didn't exactly jump up and down or open the champagne, but if Susie or Snoopy said they had had enough, and were packing up their bowls, I would be distraught. I would beg them to change their minds and then I would beg again, offering to mend my ways, or to shop more often at M&S if only they would grace me with their presence just a little bit longer.

It's just a special bond My cats have given me so much. I wonder at people who think cats are boring, that they just sit in a corner and don't do very much. That they are coy and miserly with affection. That they show no loyalty. That they are aloof and unlovable. Cats give back precisely what you give to them, and tenfold. They want to be included and consulted and talked to. You just have to learn how to communicate with them, and let them into your life.

It is no coincidence that so many of the people who have contributed to this book are writers. I think they chose that profession just so that they could stay home more, and be quiet, and think, and share cups of tea with a small, pink, raspy tongue. There is a smattering of male contributors, but on the whole the greatest lovers of cats are women. Why that is I don't really know, but I put it down to the love between human and cat not being obvious, or status driven, or showy. You have to watch a cat really closely, and get to know him or her intimately, to appreciate how special cats are. It is just a bond. As Jilly Cooper writes in her funny and affectionate contribution, 'My cats give me so much fun and laughter and affection. Watching them run down the garden towards me is a constant joy.' You really couldn't want for anything more.

Confessions of a cat woman

MAY 2007

In which we learn that cats notice every teeny, tiny thing, but never make disparaging comments. In which we discover that our cats will never leave us for someone younger and more adventurous in bed, and why Snoopy is doing his pulling-himself-along-the-bottom-of-the-sofa thing and Sweetie smells like a fish.

Why loving fur babies is the greatest love of all

When I used to come home to my husband, I never knew what mood he would be in. Grumpy. Silent. Upstairs with the 'office' (and I use the word lightly) door closed (cats and wives simply detest closed doors). On the phone (despite the fact I was actually there, in the room, after sometimes quite a long gap since we had last seen each other, my husband never once, not once, said to the person on the other end of the line, who hadn't even bothered to turn up, let alone marry him, 'Um, excuse me for a moment while I kiss my wife hello.' Oh no. That would have been too difficult and demanding. No, my husband wouldn't even acknowledge my existence but would shelter the phone in the crook of his neck and then head upstairs, sometimes making a gesture that I am pretty sure meant, Shush).

Sometimes he would be making a mess. Sometimes he would have already made the mess and be asleep, fully clothed, on top of the duvet even though it was still light outside. Sometimes he would be sitting in the kitchen with the overhead lights on, when he knows I prefer more ambient light and Diptyque candles. Alternatively, to ring the changes, he would be sitting in the kitchen in total darkness. (He could never, in seven years of living together, get the lighting quite right.) Or he might be on the internet, relentlessly checking his emails. You can tell. There was static.

Why am I writing about a horrid man when I should be writing about fur babies? Well, I am just trying to make a point. When you come home to a cat, there is always a welcome, a cheery, chirrupy, squirmy, furry one. When I open the front door, whether I have been gone for a mere five minutes to buy a paper, or a whole, long week at the fashion shows in New York or Paris or Milan, the same ritual is performed.

There is Squeaky, right by the front door, scratching away furiously on the coir doormat, rump in the air, as if to say, 'Mummy, look! Mummy, where have you been?' Halfway down the hall is Sweetie, sitting all good and straight backed, her little crooked mouth half open, her green eyes like dinner plates, before she pussy foots (there is no other way to describe it, I'm afraid) towards me to have her giant feather-duster tail pulled between my fingers. Susie is always standing, poised to scarper, tail in its habitual question mark, on the stairs down to the kitchen, looking over her elegant backside to check if it really is me, in which case she might think about not bolting straight out the cat flap. Snoopy is behind the sofa in the front room, and he will only come out to say hello (a chirrup followed by a head butt) after you have called his name. He doesn't like showing too much childish excitement.

They take turns to look after me Since my husband left (as I write this, exactly four weeks ago), it has been just me and the cats (and the fish, who keep having sex and producing tiddlers; I now have ten, in various sizes. They like to torment Sweetie by splashing at the surface and making bubbles). In that sweet cat way of theirs, they are still taking it in turns to look after me. I go to bed, and am soon joined by Squeaky (we have our face-at-the-top-of-the-precipice moment as she tries to clamber onto the duvet), and then Sweetie, who occupies the space formerly taken up by my husband.

This is a much better arrangement, to be honest. Neither puss tells me to switch the light off, or set the alarm for 6 a.m. because they want to do yoga (cats are naturally supple, and love to sleep more than anything else in the world), or turn the telly off because they hate *Sex and the City* (my cats think there should be a remake called *Sex and the Kitty*).

I have never known Sweetie to jam the duvet between her furry thighs, although she does like to knead it and create holes in my vintage linen. None of the girls keeps getting up noisily, eyes still closed with the sheer fatigue of being alive, to go for a noisy and protracted wee just when I have managed to drop off.

Then, at about four in the morning, I hear a click clack of toenails (I sleep very lightly because of the pussies, like a human mummy, well, I am human but you know what I mean), and Snoopy, probably scared and lonely and anxious, lands on my chest to spend the rest of the night dribbling on my nightie.

When I wake, the pussies – unlike my husband, who never once thought he should wake up with me, brushing a hand across my face and kissing me softly – are still there, all bright eyed and bushy tailed at the first stirring from my area, ready for breakfast. Whoever said that cats like to go hunting at night has never met mine. Even Susie, when I creep downstairs (because she doesn't like noise), is still on the elephant club chair in the sitting room, giving me a lovely yawn and a stretch.

And they still come first   My husband always knew I loved my cats more than I loved him. They always came first. I think he loved them, too, in his own strange, detached, selfish man-way, but for example he would always make himself a cup of coffee (instant!) before he prepared their breakfasts, which I thought rather mean. Now that I am husbandless and the cats are members of a single-parent broken home, we have our little routine; it is a bit like the scene in *Kramer vs Kramer* when Dustin Hoffman finally learns to make perfect French toast for his son.

The alarm goes off (which is Squeaky, who starts to lick my face and bat me with her paw), we all troop downstairs, and I get their breakfast ready before I do anything else, even switch on Radio 4. Susie sometimes joins us, but usually she likes to hover, before she decides whether to have breakfast (human breakfast, not cat breakfast) in the sitting room by her chair if it is raining or cold, or on the garden wall if it is sunny and there are no wasps about (she absolutely hates wasps). Only when they are all replete do I put the kettle on and grind my beans, apologising all the while to Susie for the noise.

I admit, though, that if I didn't have the cats I would be feeling lonely, and bereft. There would, almost, be no reason for getting up, or ordering food from Ocado (mainly 'human' cat food and non-clumping cat litter, I have to admit). There would be no need for order, or for me to get out of bed at all. But I have to put on a brave face for them, because they pick up on every vibe, every nuance of a mood. I remember the first time I found out my husband was cheating on me (Christmas Eve 2005, with Daphne, the boring New York travel agent who kept phoning him to talk about the theatre; I mean, come on). I shouted at him for the very first time, and Susie was so shocked she broke the cat flap in her panic to get out of the house.

That is no way to live. Cats hate conflict. They hate it when I cry (and I have been doing a lot of that lately). They try to cheer me up, they really do. Snoopy has been doing his pulling-himself-along-the-bottom-of-the-sofa thing, which he hasn't done in years. Squeaky has been playing with her catnip banana rather than using it as a pillow. And Sweetie fell into the pond. She has always been pretty clumsy, but the other morning she was wobbling along the upper part of the garden wall, trying to gaze down at the fish, and she fell in, and plunged right to the bottom. She managed to scramble out, but she refused to let me dry her, such was her embarrassment. She smelt vaguely fishy for about a week.

Snoopy is always there for me
I keep telling Snoopy that of all the men in my life (I say 'all', but there were only three boyfriends, two of whom didn't like me that much, and one husband, who, it turned out, didn't like me at all) he has been the only one I have been able to rely on, to trust completely, who gazes at me with shiny, loving eyes that aren't secretly thinking, I wish she was younger, and dimmer, and I could push her around a bit. Snoopy has always been there for me, uncomplaining, cheerful, affectionate. He would never cheat on me. He is such a good cat. I am sure he has some sort of special spirit; he is so kind. He seems to know everything.

When I lost my husband (well, I haven't lost him, and I certainly didn't scour the streets with a torch, several hundred leaflets and a packet of king prawns; he now lives in a sordid bedsit in Camden), I cried, a lot, but I wasn't destroyed. I hadn't lost the love of my life, because the love of my life is Snoopy. I couldn't bear to lose him. I think he knows he is the most loved cat in the world. Sometimes, he is sitting on my chest and he looks into my eyes and I swear he is telling me that everything is going to be okay, that he is there for me, and that he loves me too. I certainly never got that from my husband.

How could you leave a cat? I am sorry to go on about my husband, now my ex-husband (can you imagine having an ex-cat? A cat you no longer got on with and banished from your bed? That is unthinkable!), but I wonder how he can get up each day and not let Squeaky's otter-like tail slide through his fingers. The day I got back from holiday to find my husband had moved out, lock, stock and yoga mat, he hadn't even made sure the cats had any food. There wasn't one human tin in the cupboard, and I thought, well, that just about sums him up, doesn't it? He did love them, but not as much as I love them.

When I was in Newfoundland recently with people from the Humane Society of the United States (monitoring the annual massacre of seal pups), I met a wonderful man (no romance; don't be silly, this is a non-fiction book), a former fireman who had chosen to work with animals. The moment he heard about the hurricane in New Orleans, he put some cat baskets in the back of his truck and headed down there to try to rescue all the abandoned cats and dogs. I asked him, incredulous, how people could have left their pets behind and he said that they had been told they would only be gone a couple of days, and hadn't thought things would be so bad. Not everyone was prepared as I am, with a cat basket for each cat in an easy-to-access emergency spot.

But still. If I were asked to evacuate from Islington, I would refuse to leave without my fur babies. I wouldn't even countenance such a thought. I was reminded of all the cats and dogs in London who were evacuated during the Blitz early in the Second World War, and tried not to think of those left behind, driven mad by the noise and the chaos and the confusion. 'Susie,' I said when I got home, scratching her tiny head while she did her best Stan Laurel impression, 'what on earth would we have done with you?'

I am not alone

The most important thing is that I might be divorced (oh! The shame! I feel such a failure, so abandoned and rejected), but I am not alone. I might not have a man, but I have my cats. Unlike men (apart from Ricky Gervais, Sam Leith, Jim Davis and the other male contributors to this book, who are shamefully outnumbered by females), who fail to notice anything (new plants in the window box, a new pair of Manolo Blahniks, the fact you have just had a very painful and very embarrassing Brazilian wax to your nether regions, the fact you have lost a limb, or are dead), cats notice every teeny tiny detail.

A piece of fluff on the floor. A leaf where a leaf should not be. They notice if something is moved, even by half an inch. Even if I am sitting in a slightly unusual place – the sofa in the sitting room, say, rather than the one in the kitchen in front of the plasma screen – Sweetie will saunter in, do a double take, with an expression that says, 'What on earth are you doing there?' and be all put out and confused.

The newest, on-and-off addition to my fur family, Leo, looks, at a glance, admittedly in the dark, a lot like Squeaky, only much slimmer, without a bag that swings beneath his tummy, and a different tail. But he is completely black. And so Snoopy, on seeing him in the kitchen eating biscuits, looks at him, looks again, can't be sure, and you can see him thinking, 'Is that Squeaky or that horrid young tom cat interloper I can't stand?' He cranes his neck, unconvinced the black blob really is Squeaky. He is too old and wobbly to get close enough to find out.

Being quiet and kind and patient Am I worried about turning into a mad old cat woman? There are worse things I could be. Such as a woman who puts her new baby before her cat, though the cat was there first. Who comes round to my house and raises an eyebrow when she sees Sweetie's bottom on the bread board.

I think the thing about having a cat, as opposed to a man or a child or a dog, is that you have to be a certain type of person. You have to be quiet. And kind. And patient (oh my god, if you do choose to adopt a feral, and I hope after reading this book you are beating down the doors of the Celia Hammond Animal Trust clinics, begging to be allowed to adopt one, you will have to be so very patient, but the wait, when your feral cat does, finally, snuggle under your chin, late at night, and learns to purr, is so completely worth it).

You have to learn how to chill. You have to not worry about your Matthew Hilton Balzac sofa being shredded, or the fact there is dribble on your freshly laundered pillows (the cats', not mine). You have to learn to sit for long periods of time, with cramp in both legs, because you don't want to get up for fear of disturbing your cat in the middle of a dream.

I am so much more relaxed now that it is just me and the cats. I don't have to wear make-up or wash my hair (my cats notice, of course they do; they just don't make disparaging remarks or sneak sideways glances). I can wear tracky bottoms and a stained T-shirt for days when I am in the middle of writing something difficult. They don't care that my roots are showing, or that I haven't had my legs waxed. I don't have to worry that they are in love with someone else, someone younger and sexier and more interesting. They only care that I love them.

Fellow travellers

In which we learn about Churchill, the giant tabby who deletes computer files; Docket, the cat who thinks he is a rabbit; Lenny, the ladykiller who closely resembles Leslie Phillips; Perry, the 9/11 cat with Lassie levels of communication; Henry, the black mog whose personality is a mix of gravity and waggery; Kilburn, he of the bizarre sleeping positions; Mog, the real Mog, who loved to make a terrible face at the kitchen window; and Summer, the most explosively ugly creature you have ever seen.

My story

CELIA HAMMOND

I run three low-cost neuter clinics in London and Kent for cats and dogs belonging to people unable to afford private veterinary fees. I reckon our clinics have prevented the birth of hundreds of thousands of unwanted kittens and puppies. There are forty-nine people on the payroll, plus volunteers, manning the head office, the clinics, our 24-hour rescue service and the sanctuary. It's a very different life from the heady days I enjoyed as a top photographic model in the 1960s.

I was born in Indonesia – my father was a tea taster – and we moved to Australia when I was still a baby. Although we didn't have animals, I always loved them. My mum told me I used to rescue lizards in the park and, eventually, I was allowed to have two kittens. But when we moved again they were rehomed, and that had a terrible impact on me because I had loved them so much. I still prefer most animals to most people. I was sent to one of those boarding schools where you are locked in and never see anybody, which wasn't a very good grounding for what some people might call a 'normal' life.

I was discovered at the age of twenty-one by photographer Norman Parkinson. Jean Shrimpton and I had started at the Lucy Clayton School

of Modelling in the same week. She quickly got involved with David Bailey and began appearing on the cover of *Vogue* while I really struggled. I just didn't look the way a model was supposed to look: I was too fat and had a round, podgy face. But Norman Parkinson used to come over once or twice a year from Tobago and have these cattle markets where he would look all the girls over and he just took a fancy to me for some reason. Suddenly, all the people who had turned me down wanted me. And that was it. I went straight to the top, appearing on the covers of *Queen* and *Vogue*. I did the Paris collections soon after Parkinson discovered me, although I had to stop eating for two or three weeks before I went because I was so fat. If I tried to sneak a bit of sugar in my tea he'd rap my knuckles. And even then they had to unstitch all the clothes down the back because I couldn't get into them.

I started rescuing cats completely by chance. I was on a bus, on the way home – this must have been in the mid Sixties, when I was still modelling – and I saw a little cat's face in the window of a boarded-up house. Wondering how on earth was she going to get out, I jumped off the bus, and went to fetch my girlfriend, who lived nearby, and her boyfriend, who brought along a crowbar. We broke in, went upstairs and there was the little cat in a room with three dead kittens. She was emaciated, and I took her home with me. And that's how it all began.

I was living in a mansion block in West Hampstead and it got to the point there were so many rescued cats in my flat that there was hardly any room for me! So I decided I'd buy a little cottage in Kent for me and the cats, and commute up to London for work. By that time I had a partner, and we lived in my house for a few years, along with all the cats. Then, when he became very successful, he bought a manor house in Wadhurst in Sussex, and we moved there, taking all the cats with us.

I continued to model for a few years, but it became more and more difficult to combine modelling with rescuing cats – and sustaining a relationship. I was bored with fashion, to be honest, and modelling became more and more of an irrelevance. It was time spent away from what I wanted to do with animals. I was then involved in several campaigns about fur and factory farming.

So why do I focus on cats? Well, I have always found that sick or unhappy cats, being less conspicuous, tend to suffer more than dogs. If a dog is in trouble, everybody is aware of it: he barks, and people notice him. But when a cat is in trouble, it hides, only coming out in the middle of the night. (That isn't to say we don't rescue dogs. We have a little puppy in at the moment whose owner went out leaving her on the top of a pair of bunk beds. The puppy fell off, breaking her leg, and trauma to her head has caused blindness in both eyes.) Secondly, although a lot of the animals we rescue live in dreadful circumstances, in my experience cats are remarkably stoical, brave and selfless. Many mother cats put their own lives at risk to rear their kittens. One mother cat, who was like a walking skeleton, carried a chicken bone across a main road to the kittens she had hidden in the basement of a shop. And, finally, I just think that there's something compelling about an animal that will only give itself to you if it wants to.

Take, for example, a cat called Gummy we have in at the moment. She had kittens in the front garden of a house in East London and neighbours told us that the kittens were discovered by a group of children, who picked them up and ran off with them. The kittens must have come to grief, as they were only two days old and couldn't possibly have survived without their mother. Gummy was very distressed and had wandered the streets for days calling for them. We caught her but, although we have tried to get through to her, she cannot bring herself to trust anyone. We think she would be happier in an environment such as a stable or smallholding, where she need not live so close to people.

We rehomed over three thousand cats last year. Those we can't home live the remainder of their lives in the freedom and comfort of our twelve-acre sanctuary in the Sussex countryside. For some elderly feral cats with disabilities or health problems needing daily medication, release at the sanctuary is not practical. It's becoming increasingly difficult to find suitable foster homes for such cats, so we are wiring off a quarter-acre secure enclosure where they will be able to sleep in heated cabins, snooze in the grass and just generally chill out. It'll be lovely for them.

I don't keep any of the cats we rescue, not even the special ones. Like Churchill, a great big gentle bear of a tabby who sits in the clinic's reception and steals people's pens and deletes files on the computer. He was a stray, living in people's gardens, hoping someone would take him in, and when he arrived he was covered in abscesses. I would love to have him but he needs a home where someone can give him day-in, day-out security; I am away from home far too much, scrambling around on building sites or in factories, trapping feral or injured cats.

I wanted to keep all the cats I rescued when I was living with my ex-partner. That's one of the reasons we broke up. Now I live above the clinic in Canning Town – well, it is just a bed in a room – and I don't actually want another relationship. I was heartbroken when my long-term relationship finished, but at the end of the day I don't want someone asking me, 'What time are you going to be back? Where are you going?' And I'm glad I never had children. I'm not a baby person. But I'm so busy I haven't got time to be lonely.

Sometimes, though, I feel as if we are trying to empty a bath with a teaspoon. The people who upset me most are those who love animals but who just don't get the fact that it's not a good idea to let a dog or a cat have a litter. Very intelligent people will say, 'Look, it's our cat. We're worried about our cat. We're not worried about other people's cats.' How can they think like that? Bring five kittens into the world and you condemn five kittens in a shelter to death. We get calls several times a day from people saying, 'Unless you come and get these kittens/cats now, I'm throwing them out.' And then there are the calls from workmen on building sites, and refuse workers who find litters of kittens in dustbins.

I do wonder sometimes whether I am actually achieving anything. You give up your whole life yet have you really made a difference? But you just come back and have a cup of tea and you get over it. If I feel

CHURCHILL

CHURCHILL

like that, I ring up one of the other rescue workers and say, 'I'm really down. Can you talk to me for a little while?'

You would not believe how much cruelty there is in Canning Town. It's mostly the kids. They've all got these Staffies with studded harnesses and they stand on street corners saying, 'Don't touch it! I'm trying to make him fierce!' This is the dog-fighting capital of London. We get cats who have been set upon by dogs, and lots and lots of cats who have been shot. You get the feeling that this generation is beyond help. I was beaten up by a young girl outside the nightclub two doors down the other night. It was 5 a.m., the nightly noise was, as usual, deafening, and I was so desperate for sleep I went outside and said, 'Could you turn that down? I've got to start work in two hours.' And this girl kicked me up the backside and I went flying. It is absolutely awful here. We could move. We could operate our clinics in nicer areas but the animals here really need us. And so this is where we have to be.

It is so nice of you to give me a manicure Pumpkin, ... I always remember, back in the 60's, how Celia used to spend hours each week putting on her false nails so that she looked just perfect for the camera.... By the way, Bart is next......

yes. Puff Puff meow!

GRACE CODDINGTON
Pumpkin, Bart and me

Oh Pumpkin dear — you look so pretty in that John Galliano coat — I hear you want to be a "supermodel".... did you know that our Mother and Celia Hammond were good friends and modeled together in the 1960's .....? Bart and I would like to enter you for "America's next top model" .... what do you think ....?

AMANDA BRUNS

New York City in the winter glistens with ice and snow and it can sometimes feel as though you are living within a giant snow globe. Steam rises from the streets and people become nothing but two eyeballs peering through layers of wool and polyester blends. However, when you are struggling with a severe head cold and stuck outside in minus-five-degree wind chill it can be a bleak and grey hell. In late November 2004, while urgently wiping my runny nose on my jacket sleeve outside Giorgio Armani,

my focus on getting from point A to point B as quickly as possible was interrupted by a panicked woman talking wildly on her cell phone and staring at a cardboard box on the side walk. My curiosity got the better of me and I stopped to find out what was going on.

A note was taped to the top of the damp box. It read, 'ABANDONED KITTY, PLEASE TAKE HOME.' My heart dropped straight to my stomach. Surely, no one would leave a cat outside in a cardboard box in this weather? I peeled

AMANDA WITH KILALA

AMI (BRADLY'S CAT)

back the taped lid and peaked inside. As light sneaked into the box, a tiny kitten came into focus. Scared and cold, it had been left with no blankets, no food and no water. The woman on the cell phone had been trying to find a home for the kitten and was relieved when I scooped up the box and headed for my train back to Brooklyn. I told her I already had the perfect name for my new kitten, Kilala.

After a short train ride that seemed like eternity, I got the box'o'kitten to my apartment. My boyfriend Bradly and I immediately opened it up and were met by the two beautiful green eyes of one tiny eight-week-old kitten. She was terrified, and spent the next several hours trying to hide. We wrapped her in a warm blanket and I sat with her in my arms for hours. We took turns comforting her during the night.

It was months before she built up enough courage to walk freely around the apartment. As she relaxed and settled into her new home she exploded with personality. She soon spent her nights 'making biscuits' in my hair and sucking on my earlobes. Tangled hair and wet earlobes are a small price to pay for true love.

BRADLY BROWN

At 7.35 a.m. the alarm on my cell phone hits its high note. Although my first instinct is to throw the small blinking and screaming piece of plastic across my room, I usually just crawl out of bed and head towards the bathroom. When I finally wake up enough to focus my eyes it's 8.15 a.m. and I'm out the door to work. Five minutes later and I'm standing in line to get the best soy cappuccino in Brooklyn at Champion Coffee. I hold the hot paper cup in my hands as if it were liquid gold, and head straight out into the brisk fall air.

It's about a fifteen-minute walk across the bridge to the 7 train. My eyes are now half open after the first few sips of coffee and I cut through the residential streets to avoid people. The first street I head down is usually calm and I take my time walking. About halfway down the block I am stopped in my tracks. A big blue, Recyclables Only garbage can has begun to squeak at me. By now

I have woken up a little more and know that garbage cans usually don't squeak, unless provoked. Refocusing my eyes a bit lower, on the ground, I see a small black and white kitten pop her head out from around the blue dumpster.

She looked about three months old and was very happy to find a potential new friend. She ran over to my feet as I squatted down to pet her. She was soft, too soft for a street cat I thought. So, after a quick scratch, I started to head for work, but I wasn't going to get away that easily. This kitten followed me down the block, keeping up with my pace, like she knew where I was going. Eventually she stopped before I got to my subway station, gave me a few squeaks goodbye and headed back to her trashcans.

The next day it was the same routine: alarm, shower, coffee and kitten. And the next. Every morning she would pop out at the same place and walk with me almost all the way to Queens. The next week I had to show Amanda my new best friend. We went to get a cappuccino and look for the kitten. Amanda and I weren't sure if she was truly a stray or just perhaps a rare indoor/outdoor city kitty. However, she wasn't there. We agreed to try again a few days later

and, sure enough, there she was. We checked for a collar or signs of spaying or neutering but there was nothing. Amanda scooped her up and just kept walking, back to our apartment, hoping the new kitten and Kilala would become fast friends.

Unfortunately, it was not love at first sight, but the kitten was determined to win Kilala over. We named our new family member Ami. After a few weeks of daily medication, a couple of baths, and a few train rides to the vet, Ami was no longer a dumpster-diving street cat. She was a spoiled-rotten, playful, fluffy kitten.

Now, Ami and Kilala play all day and take naps with each other in the big brown chair, although you'll still be hard pressed to get Kilala to admit that. I also have no need for an alarm anymore, since I'm woken up every morning at 7.35 a.m. by a big ball of fluff and a little wet tongue.

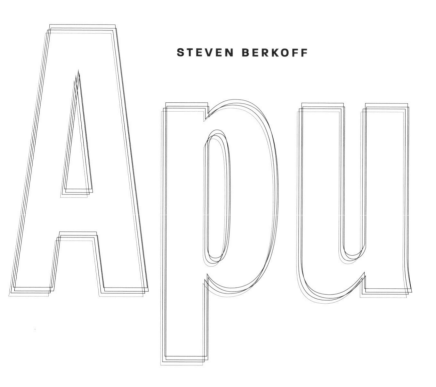

STEVEN BERKOFF

I've always had cats except for a twenty-year period when it wasn't appropriate and we had sour ever-complaining neighbours who would have made it impossible. But they happily left in the end and we bought a fancy Bengal kitten.

I'm basically happy with moggies and since childhood I'd collected strays and brought them home. Stepney was full of strays then, and Mum and I had such pleasure watching their incredible antics. At one time we had about five of them running around and it could get quite crowded in our two rooms but the pleasure their company gave us made up for the rather bleak surroundings.

My first cat was called Peter and came with the house we rented during the war in Luton. I grew very fond of him, a beautiful, silky black cat, but one day the owners turned up to take him away. It was a terrible shock and I broke down completely. However, some weeks later Peter found his own way back to us, thin and hungry, after a five-mile journey! He immediately climbed onto the kitchen cabinet and hauled down a piece of fried fish intended for our supper but we were all so amazed and moved to see him that we could only gasp in wonder.

During my Islington years I was given a cat to mind while the owner, Eliza Ward, an actress, was in rep but by the time she came back the cat and I were firm friends and Eliza just left her with me. I had that cat, called Pottle (Eliza's choice), for seventeen years. She was a beautiful tortoiseshell and a highly intelligent animal. But one winter I was away in rep and my tenant, who I had asked to take care of her, left her out on a freezing night, and she died. I was horrified and miserable.

We got the Bengal kitten after my partner became ill, had a serious operation and then slowly recovered and rather craved a Bengal cat. We had seen them featured in magazines. (The Bengal is a strange kind of beast which has been bred down from the Asian Leopard Cat over a period of years and now they have just about got it right.) When we bought him, he yelled all the way home but as soon as he got indoors, he sniffed around, settled and later went to his dirt box without fuss. My partner called him Apu, after Satyajit Ray's Apu film trilogy, of which she is very fond, and after all he is a bit oriental.

He is a most extraordinary creature, as the booklet that accompanied him suggested he might be. That he is awesomely beautiful is beyond question and he possesses abundant energy, running with an amazing bounce and frequently demanding to be played with. He is also inordinately affectionate.

Any animal changes the atmosphere of a home somehow. It's as if it poured a soothing vibration into it or maybe wove itself into your lives, giving you another strand, another colour, in the weft and warp of your daily actions. But this cat is unique in its relationship with us because he seeks human attention almost obsessively and that need finds greatest expression in his extraordinary desire to communicate vocally.

He is now able to make himself understood with a whole cacophony of sounds. If both of us have been out for a few hours, we are often met with half a dozen cries of delight, relief, excitement or even jubilation! Then he settles. But my partner seems to be able to pick up his rhythm so when she asks him something the little beast appears to understand the very core of the question and respond. The effect is startling.

Perhaps these Bengals are just a few million brain cells smarter than their fellow moggies. The 'speaking' varies from day to day but some days it becomes quite intense and it's usually only between my partner and the cat since he has a very strong relationship with her.

Cat owners can be, or seem to be, boring or simple loonies to 'real' people with real problems and responsibilities. But you can develop a deep affection for an animal, just as you might for a child, and I see nothing wrong or sinful in that since I am no less fond of children. Love for a harmless, dependent creature can be a special thing, bringing many hours of warmth. And, apart from that, cats are so damned beautiful!

Rattle, Tilson-Thomas, Bonnie & Clyde, and Feral

JILLY COOPER

At present I have four cats: black and white and very fluffy Rattle who must be about twelve, who was named after the conductor Simon Rattle because they both look rather glamorous and fuzzy haired. Rattle had a brother called Tilson-Thomas, named after the conductor Michael Tilson-Thomas. Michael is very sleek and dark haired and pale faced and short haired like Tilson-Thomas the cat.

Rattle and Tilson-Thomas were utterly devoted to each other, and played and romped all day. Tilson used to come for walks with me through the woods and adored KitKat and was the most extrovertly loving and charming cat. Rattle his brother is very shy, and skitters around. He is rather like a married man; he avoids you and pretends he doesn't know you exist in public, and then is all over you in private, particularly in bed. He has an adorable habit of coming into bed with you with the dawn dew on his paws, and snuggling up to you and purring his head off.

He has a less attractive habit, because he is a wool fetishist, of taking flying leaps onto your back with claws out when you are wearing cashmere and on the telephone. He also leaps onto your bare back when you are on the telephone. He loves to sit on the old-fashioned oblong radiator downstairs (which is known as Rattle's flat) with both front paws stuck out. He likes to have breakfast, chopped chicken, in bed in his flat.

Tragically, around 1994, my housekeeper Jane, who was living in the cottage at the bottom of the drive, left. She also left a husband, several dogs and two cats, Bonnie and Clyde, whom I inherited. Bonnie and Clyde are lovely but total thugs, black with white shirt fronts, and they took over and saw off poor Tilson and Rattle, who never had quite the same happy relaxed life again. But, having taken on Bonnie and Clyde, I had to stick with them.

Bonnie is a great purrer and a great hisser and a complete pig. She spends a lot of the day eating and her tummy trails on the ground when she walks. She is also very affectionate. Clyde is sweet, very long legged with huge whiskers, and a pig too, but not as much as Bonnie. Clyde talks back to you with miaows when you talk to him. I feel ashamed that, like a stepmother, I always pay a little less attention to them than I do to Rattle.

When Clyde and Bonnie came to live with us they were joined by my housekeeper's black Labrador, Bessie, who was a heavenly dog. They all adored each other and worked as a pack. When Bessie had a stroke, all our cats formed a guard of honour around her and wouldn't leave her side until she had recovered. They were heart broken when she died about four years ago, leaving us with one lurcher, Hero, who preserved a kind of armed neutrality with all the cats.

About two years before Bessie died, however, there were rumours of a black panther in the area. People kept seeing him, and I caught sight of a large black animal in the woods on several occasions. Finally, I rang up the local paper, who did a 'Jilly sees black panther' story. Later I had to ring up in embarrassment to say I had got a closer sighting of the

'panther' and he was actually a long-haired, fluffed-out (because it was bleak midwinter) black cat.

I kept seeing him all over the valley, and he always fled. I felt so sorry for him that I started putting saucers of food in our barn, about two hundred and fifty yards from our house. Soon I was feeding him twice a day. I used to see his big yellow eyes peering out of the woods and the moment I left he would thud into the barn. Gradually he came closer and closer, until the heavenly day when I first held him purring in my arms.

After about eighteen months, I called him Feral. Feral started appearing at windows, mewing, and finally after two years he decided to move in. This was too much for Bessie the Labrador, who didn't want her position, as chief rescuee, usurped. Bessie led a posse of Bonnie and Clyde into the room where we store all our drink and tried to bump off Feral. Feral retreated to the woods until the day Bessie died and then, led by Rattle, moved in.

Like all usurpers, he took a few days to suss out the pecking order. He then made friends with Clyde and Rattle, is polite to Bonnie, because he doesn't like being hissed at, and started bullying the life out of poor Tilson-Thomas. Endless dreadful yowling fights took place all over the house for the next year and a half, and no matter how many glasses of water I threw at Feral, he wouldn't stop bullying poor Tilson, who got thinner and thinner. The vet diagnosed a very overactive thyroid, and poor darling Tilson, purring to the end, was finally put down just before Christmas. It broke all our hearts, except perfidious Feral and Rattle, who have chummed up and are now inseparable.

Feral, I have to say, is the best and funniest cat I've ever met. He behaves just like a dog, following me all round the garden, and is devastated if I set out on my rounds feeding the birds (two different tables) and the fish in the morning without him. He also sits on the stairs waiting for me to come home and sulks if I wash my hair as he knows I am going out.

He lies in your arms like a baby, and sleeps in a milk crate while I'm working in the gazebo at the bottom of the garden. He adores taking flying leaps into what everyone is doing, landing on laps, laptops, the post, the bills when they are being paid, and he loves shredding newspapers. We all love him to bits.

He was delighted when our old lurcher died at Christmas 2002 and took over as honorary dog. Then he was absolutely furious (all the cats were) when I acquired a greyhound called Father, from Ireland, in June 2006. The greyhound, however, who had been appallingly cruelly treated, is the gentlest, sweetest creature in the world, far more frightened of the cats than they are of him. So now they all try and sleep on our bed, and get on extremely well.

Feral is still a bit beady, and you have to make sure he gets a great deal of fuss. If any strange dogs come to the house, he takes off in umbrage to my son and daughter-in-law's house a hundred yards down the road.

Although I adore my cats, I was ashamed how they blossomed in the eighteen months between Hero the lurcher's death and the greyhound's arrival. Like all animals, they flourish with love and attention.

They are dreadfully faddy, and have chicken and coley, gourmet sachets and all sorts of goodies cooked for them. The only time I don't love them is in the early morning when they mew their heads off to be fed, and turn down everything I give them, so I have to tip the lot into a bowl for the badgers, and start all over again.

But they give me so much fun and laughter and affection. Watching them run down the garden towards me is a constant joy.

DOCKET

Tracey Emin

I have said this many times before but
when I wake up in the morning and see
his little grey and white face, long
white whiskers, little black nose, big
round eyes and fluffy ears, I can't
believe that God could have made
something so perfect. I can't convey
to many human beings, unless they are
cat lovers, how much I love Docket.
      People think that cats are aloof
and cold. Docket is the complete
opposite. He is very cuddly, talks a
lot and can actually follow a couple
of commands. Often when I go to bed at
night I am carrying a tray with hot
milk, a jug of water, a glass and maybe
a newspaper. One thing for sure is
that I can't carry Docket up five
flights of stairs to the bedroom too –
that was a habit he got used to when he
was a kitten. Now, I place the tray on
the bottom of the stairs, I clap my
hands and in a high-pitched voice
I say, 'Up!' As he gallops up each
flight, I can hear myself saying,
'Mummy loves you!'
      Often in the morning he will wake
me up, either by puddy pawing around
on the bed, or banging on his tin of
IAMS like a drum. And what's really
funny about this is that when I open
the tin and place the food in his bowl,

DOCKET SAys HIGH MICE x
INocents - Fleabite - Misty -
Maley - Charlie - OR Moonies
I Love you ALL.

FOR MISS HAMMOND f

Tracy Emin x

he feigns a lack of interest. But
then, if I 'carelessly' spill some
outside the bowl and say in a high-
pitched voice, 'Ooops!', he gobbles
everything up.

He has a number of hobbies. One
is opening cupboard doors. Another is
standing on his hind legs facing the
corner of a room and just kind of
mincing his front paws like a rabbit.
He's been doing this since he was
about eight months old. And it was a
while before I found out that one of my
neighbours had a rabbit. She told me
they would have great fun watching
this rather slow grey and white cat
sit for hours imitating the rabbit!
His other hobby, of which I am
extremely proud, is making sculptures
out of cardboard boxes.

You take an ordinary cardboard
box (say, 2 feet by 1 foot 6 inches),
fold the lid in on itself, and make a
small hole in one of the sides. It's at
this point that Docket starts tearing
at the hole with his teeth so that it's
big enough for him to get in. And this
is the really clever bit – he then
tears the cardboard from the inside,
using his mouth to fling the chewed-
off pieces across the kitchen as far
as he can like some bowerbird until he
has actually fashioned the right shape
for a comfortable head rest.

Docket is half British Blue and
half moggy. He came from Vallance
Road, where the Kray twins came from.
The only thing that Docket seems to

have in common with them is that he is
a touch on the dandy side. His best
friend was Fleebite – a strange little
creature with greasy fur and no teeth
– whose last couple of years, after a
trip to the vet and the kindness of
Celia Hammond, was spent in comfort
with Docket in a much healthier state.
Docket's new best friend is a camp
little ginger thing called Pious who
lives a few doors down.

My quality of life is now a
million times better, thanks to
Docket. Unconditional love is so
important in this world.

LENNY THE LION

BETHAN COLE

In the summer of 2001 I lost something very precious. Three months later, the black clouds of depression started to lift and a furry young alpha male called Lenny sauntered into my life. Lenny was an orphan, a foundling, a wastrel. We first set eyes upon him one grey October day at Battersea Dogs' Home, my brother and I. He was my brother's thirtieth birthday present to me – my birthday fell at the end of September.

There were many cats that day lined up in their even rows of cages. One poorly cat who'd had all his head shaved after an operation – he was quickly taken. A little white eight-month-old female who had a rather delicate look about her and was sleeping – she was my favourite.

A big, old venerable tabby – also taken. 'He looks like he would be called Lenny,' observed my brother of this big old boy. Then we saw another one, a nine-month-old neutered male tabby, whose cage bore the legend Gremlin. 'He's going to grow up to be like old Lenny, isn't he?' my brother said. My brother Neil wanted to buy young Lenny for me. But Lenny the younger, whose original name was Diamond (for some reason I imagined he was a proud working-class boy who had come from a South London council block with ruched blinds and a white leather three-piece suite) was taken, so we continued browsing the cattery. Then suddenly the people who'd decided to bag young Lenny changed their minds. He was ours! Neil paid £25.

We put Lenny in a box and sped home in a minicab. I'll always remember opening the cardboard box in my flat and how confidently and elegantly he eased himself out, as though nothing had happened and he'd lived there all his life. We put down some Iams in his little Battersea Dogs' Home bowl and a saucer of milk, and Lenny made himself at home. It soon became apparent that (like me) Lenny had a few behavioural problems. When 'over stimulated' or disturbed during sleep, he would sink his teeth into my fat pink leg or arm and cling on like a limpet, until extreme pain caused me to prise him off. Hence Gremlin, I suppose. He took great pleasure in puncturing and scratching to pieces my Liberty leather sofa. But most days he was quite loving and would lie in my lap whilst I read or watched TV. If you were very lucky, he would roll on his back and expose his treacle-coloured spotty tummy to be fondled and smoothed.

My boyfriend at the time, the owner of six cats whose names all began with the letter B (he fancied himself as a latter-day William Burroughs), discerned a kind of Leslie Phillips demeanour in Lenny's ladykiller manoeuvres. Lenny would slink about, using languid movements of body and tail to dictate to his servile human (me) that he needed food, adoration, pampering, treats, toilet trips. Lenny had polyamorous proclivities. One woman (me) was not enough and he soon found a feline girlfriend too, a dainty little black and white thing that would appear at the french window of my living room each night and wait patiently for Lenny to join her on night-time escapades. How very T.S. Eliot, I thought, and imagined them dancing by the light of the moon or the sodium glare of a street lamp.

In February 2003 Lenny had a strange 'accident'. I discovered him one morning on my balcony wrapped in a blanket I had been drying outside. He was dragging the back half of his body and it appeared to have collapsed under him. On closer inspection his leg had a bloody puncture wound, like he'd been stamped on with a stiletto, and obviously something was broken. I whipped him down to the vets at Mile End. The vet, a handsome blonde Australian man, whose gentleness in handling Lenny was heart-melting, thought he might have been knocked down by a car. Lenny's hip was dislocated. But I was suspicious. How then had Lenny subsequently dragged himself back from the road and wrapped himself in a blanket? Most odd. I have my theories.

Lenny had to have an operation, which cost £600. He came home after a day or two and all of his hindquarters had been shaved. He was like a little pink rabbit. Very lovable and vulnerable. He lay below the radiator in my living room, immobilised on the little scrap of patchwork blanket we'd brought him home from Battersea on, and we nursed him back to health, with tasty morsels and Whiskas cat milk.

By the end of 2004 I was travelling a lot with work, my brother had moved from London to Cornwall, and there was no one to look after Lenny when I went away. That November, my mother offered to take Lenny in whilst I visited a spa in Bora Bora for ten days. And so Lenny was airlifted up to my mother's terraced house in Shrewsbury. Like Madonna, swooping down to Malawi and scooping up little David Banda in her arms, she came to save Lenny from his harsh urban life on the mean borders of Hackney and Tower Hamlets. Lenny, as my friend Sarah observed, had been 'taken into care'. It was meant to be temporary, but three years later there he still is. My mother and he have become inseparable – it's tough love though. She has tamed his behavioural problems; she feeds him about ten meals a day. Consequently Lenny now cuts a slightly portly figure and has recently been ordered by the vet to lose some weight.

Lenny has new friends in Shropshire. He catches voles and toads and mice every night and eyes up the bird table with an incessant and unappeasable hunger. His next-door neighbour is a semi-feral creature called Ceri, a small, fierce farmhouse cat with long silky hair. He quickly subordinated her. Shropshire is like a theme park for animals: it's alive with squirrels and hedgehogs and ribbiting frogs. Lenny is transfixed by them all. There aren't many animals around where I live now, apart from the Staffordshire bull terriers who dart about Victoria Park. Yet some summer evenings, when I look out of my french windows, I see a little black and white cat on the grass outside. It is Lenny's old girlfriend, coming to see if he's back.

Garfield
and other cats

I grew up on a small farm near Fairmount, Indiana. We raised milch cows, which are cattle raised for their milk. The farming operation was simple with a staff that included Mom, Dad, my younger brother, Davy, and me. Every day there were chores, including pitching hay and shovelling manure. It was humble, but a good way for a kid to learn about the value of hard work.

Like most farms, there were always cats around. I'm sure my parents never bought a cat – the cats just migrated toward the shelter of the barn, and multiplied. At one time, we counted twenty-five cats.

One of my favourite cats on the farm was Granny. I'd originally named her Tom until she had a litter of kittens. I didn't get around to renaming her until after her kittens had kittens, hence, Granny. Days before she had each litter, she'd show me where she'd prepared her bed in the hayloft or a manger. I always kept her in milk and food as she tended her young.

All our cats were 'barn cats'. They were mousers. Granny was always going into the corncribs or the fields and bringing back mice for her kittens. Our cats were rugged and fearless hunters, unlike Garfield.

I left the farm to go off to college when I was eighteen. I majored in art, because by that time I knew I wanted to be a cartoonist. You see, when I was young, I had asthma so bad that at times I was bedridden for weeks. And lying in a prone position is the worse thing an asthmatic can do, so I was always propped up in a sitting position. During that time, my mom used to shove a pencil and paper in my hands and tell me to draw something to entertain myself. At first, I was so bad I had to label everything. I'd draw a cow and then write 'COW' beneath it with an arrow pointing to it, otherwise the cow could have easily been mistaken for a dog. Eventually my drawing improved and I found that putting captions with my drawings was far more entertaining than just the drawings themselves.

My first attempt at my own comic strip was Gnorm Gnat, based on... well, a gnat. Editors at the syndicates thought I had something, but bugs? Who can relate to a bug? So, I took a very calculated look at the comic pages and noticed there were a lot of dogs doing quite well. There was Snoopy, Belvedere, and Marmaduke – but no cats! I was inspired to create the quintessential cat, based on the memories of all the cats I grew up with.

There was a lot of diversity in the barn cats. Some were aggressive and played rough; others were content to just lie back and observe. Some were very lovable, demanding to have their tummies rubbed and their ears scratched, while others wouldn't give you the time of day. Garfield is a little of all those cats. He has a lot of attitude, but he does have a softer side, too, particularly when it comes to his teddy bear, Pooky. The name Garfield came from my Grandfather, James Garfield Davis, who was kind of a gruff old guy who also had a softer side.

At the art studio where we create Garfield, a cat – a great orange cartoon cat – is always around. He takes a lot of care and feeding, but at least he doesn't shed. We used to have a big black cat named Otto. Otto was the community cat – he could always count on someone on the staff feeding and petting him. When it got unbearably cold, someone would take him home for the night. Sometimes he'd disappear for days – and about the time we'd start worrying about him, he'd show up again. He's still around, but he spends most of his time with a neighbour now that he's older and a bit less adventurous.

The cat I have now is named Spunky. She spends most of her time in the greenhouse in my studio. She has the run of the place – she goes out when she wants, comes in when she wants, and pretty much has the world by the tail. In the winter, her name changes to 'Chunky' because she's not as inclined to run around when there's three feet of the snow on the ground and she packs on a little extra weight. Spunky is an American Shorthair – unlike Garfield, she eats cat food instead of lasagne, and sips water instead of coffee.

Cats are interesting, entertaining creatures, but you have to accept them on their own terms.

PERRY & JUNIOR

EMMA FORREST

Perry is white, Junior is orange.

This cat devotion may all trace back to a false memory: Mum took me to see *Cats* when I was six (true) and during the intermission Brian Blessed stayed on stage, in character as Old Deuteronomy, and little children were allowed to go up and meet him (true). And I went up to meet him still clinging to my box of Maltesers (true) and I dropped some on the stage and when the play resumed two dancing cats slipped on my Maltesers and died (not true).

Are my boys the reincarnation of the cats I fake killed? As I type this, Junior is staring at me from the foot of the bed with the hooded gaze and self-satisfied girth of Tony Soprano (he was named, in fact, for Tony's Uncle Junior because he, like Uncle Junior, was found wandering, confused, under a New Jersey bridge). I also named him Junior because I wanted Perry to know that he'd remain the alpha cat, my Maddox Jolie, even with a newly adopted brother. He has. Indeed Perry has been out since the crack of dawn looking for lizards to relieve of their tails and bumble bees to verbally harass.

We moved to the Hollywood Hills from New York City a year ago. All Manhattan cats are apartment cats. Our studio, on the seventeenth floor, with windows that overlooked the Empire State Building but which we couldn't open, offered them a particularly limited existence. Being in nature, with lots of land to be explored, has been transformative for Perry's personality and therefore mine, too.

Junior still lives, as he did in New York, almost entirely under the bed (we say he keeps an office there). Unless it's just me in the house and then he lives inside the crook of my elbow or under my armpit or on my forehead. Once, when I was doing push-ups, and Junior climbed on my back, I asked my boyfriend if Junior maybe thought I was his mother. 'Maybe? I think he knows you are his mother.'

EMMA WITH JUNIOR

JUNIOR

I love Perry because he is so incredibly smart – not only Lassie levels of communication but also, I suspect, retractable opposable thumbs, given that he is not only able to pull the sheets down when I try and hide from him in the morning, but also capable of turning door knobs. He has so much he needs to get done every day. Then again, I love Junior because he is so incredibly dumb and lazy.

Last week he ran under the bed because he thought I had climbed under the covers holding a monster that wanted to eat him. Then he realised that the monster was actually an ice-cream sandwich and he wanted to eat IT, and he had to come sheepishly out as if nothing uncool had happened. In summer, he lies on his back in front of the air conditioning, fanning his testicles. When he's thirsty, he lays flat on his tummy whilst he laps at the bowl. Drinking that way means that he doesn't have to bend.

I adopted them both from the same place, a year apart (Perry was a 9/11 cat; his owner never came home), and was given lots of advice about how to introduce them to each other (poor Junior was shut in the bathroom for a day). When they met, they sat next to each other on the sofa, but both stared straight into space like guests with nothing to say to each other at a cocktail party. The next day Perry started licking his new brother like crazy, whilst Junior stared stony faced, until Perry bit him, hard, on the rump. The vet said it was because he felt humiliated at not having his affection returned. Like me over the years! 'I love you' (silence). 'I love you' (blank stare). 'I hate you!' (smack!).

When we lived in the seventeenth-floor studio, Perry would sit all day in the top rung of his carpet tree, solemn and staring, looking for all the world like a news reader. For exercise we'd let them wander all the way up to the end of the hall, then we'd call the elevator and they'd come racing back to the apartment as soon as they heard the 'ping!'

Now Perry explores our acres. He tramples vegetation, races butterflies, meditates with hummingbirds, slumbers in suntraps and then is brought home by the sound of rattled food at 5 p.m. on the dot. There are coyotes here at dusk. But neighbours tell me it's the owls that really get cats. There are also other outdoor cats to be avoided: the neighbourhood tough guy called Frodo, who likes to slip under our fence and hiss. There is also a tiny half cat called Kiwi, whose owner once awoke to find her lying on the pillow next to him, nonchalantly chewing the head off a rat. Down the street is Pete, a cross-eyed tuxedo cat. And across the street there are some pet goats; one of them likes my English accent so much that he got stuck on his own roof trying to follow the sound of my voice. Then all the cats had to come out and see what he was doing.

Living with all these cats everywhere, especially the two in my bed, definitely affects my personality. Late in life, I've come to love sun bathing. I nap whenever they tell me to, which is every day from two to four. When they're in deep-space hyper purr, I too can meditate. Most importantly, I want to be loved and hugged and petted all the time, except for when I don't want it and then I not only flinch from my boyfriend's embrace but also hiss.

CHEWA

Anais Gallagher

My mum promised we could have a cat when we moved from the country to London. I just love cats. My grandma and granddad have two and I like to see them sleeping in a room on a carpet or a chair. Everything looks so homely then.

Mum took me to Harrods' pet department and I chose a very noisy Lilac Point Siamese. It took me some time to understand that when he was patrolling the house yelling his head off and stamping up and down the stairs he wasn't angry. He was just being a naughty Siamese. The kittens' mother did not have enough milk, so he had been bottle fed by the time he was mine. He was happy to be handled and cuddled.

The question of a name was the next decision to be made. I called him Our Kid for a few days, and later on Blue, and then he ended up as Chewa. Chewa loves to be held and stroked and petted and most of all he loves to sleep on my bed. I love to wake in the morning and feel the warmth and weight of Chewa on my legs and feel him purring as I touch his head, which is his sign that he is contented.

HENRY

SAM LEITH

Christopher Smart was quite mad, but he loved cats. Here's what he wrote about his cat in his poem 'Jubilate Agno'. He was born in 1722 and died in 1771. And he was quite – meaning absolutely – mad: but what he says about cats is, to this day, mostly true.

> For I will consider my Cat Jeoffrey.
> For he is the servant of the Living God, duly and daily serving him.
> For at the First glance of the glory of God in the East he worships in his way.
> For this is done by wreathing his body seven times round with elegant quickness.
> For then he leaps up to catch the musk, which is the blessing of God upon his prayer.
> For he rolls upon prank to work it in.
> For having done duty and received blessing he begins to consider himself.
> For this he performs in ten degrees.
> For first he looks upon his fore-paws to see if they are clean.
> For secondly he kicks up behind to clear away there.

For thirdly he works it upon stretch with the fore-paws
extended.
For fourthly he sharpens his paws by wood.
For fifthly he washes himself.
For sixthly he rolls upon wash.
For Seventhly he fleas himself, that he may not be
interrupted upon the beat.
For Eighthly he rubs himself against a post.
For Ninthly he looks up for his instructions.
For Tenthly he goes in quest of food.
For having consider'd God and himself he will consider
his neighbour.
For if he meets another cat he will kiss her in kindness.
For when he takes his prey he plays with it to give it a
chance.
For one mouse in seven escapes by his dallying.
For when his day's work is done his business more
properly begins.
For he keeps the Lord's watch in the night against the
adversary.
How he counteracts the powers of darkness by his
electrical skin and glaring eyes.
For he counteracts the Devil, who is death, by brisking
about the life.
For in his morning orisons he loves the sun and the sun
loves him.
For he is of the tribe of Tiger.
For the Cherub Cat is a term of the Angel Tiger.
For he has the subtlety and hissing of a serpent, which in
goodness he suppresses.
For he will not do destruction, if he is well fed, neither
will he spit without provocation.
For he purrs in thankfulness, when God tells him he's a
good Cat.
For he is an instrument for the children to learn
benevolence upon.
For every house is incomplete without him and a blessing
is lacking in the spirit.
For the Lord commanded Moses concerning the cats at
the departure of the Children of Israel from Egypt.
For every family had one cat at least in the bag.

For the English Cats are the best in Europe.

For he is the cleanest in the use of his fore-paws of any
quadrupede.

For the dexterity of his defence is an instance of the love of
God to him exceedingly.

For he is the quickest to his mark of any creature.

For he is tenacious of his point.

For he is a mixture of gravity and waggery.

For he knows that God is his Saviour.

For there is nothing sweeter than his peace when at rest.

For there is nothing brisker than his life in motion.

For he is of the Lord's poor and so indeed is he called by
benevolence perpetually – Poor Jeoffrey! poor Jeoffrey!
the rat has bit thy throat.

For I bless the name of the Lord Jesus that Jeoffrey is
better.

For the divine spirit comes about his body to sustain it in
complete cat.

For his tongue is exceedingly pure so that it has in purity
what it wants in music.

For he is docile and can learn certain things.

For he can set up with gravity which is patience upon
approbation.

For he can fetch and carry, which is patience in
employment.

For he can jump over a stick which is patience upon proof
positive.

For he can spraggle upon waggle at the word of command.

For he can jump from an eminence into his master's
bosom.

For he can catch the cork and toss it again.

For he is hated by the hypocrite and miser.

For the former is affraid of detection.

For the latter refuses the charge.

For he camels his back to bear the first notion of business.

For he is good to think on, if a man would express himself
neatly.

For he made a great figure in Egypt for his signal services.

For he killed the Ichneumon-rat very pernicious by land.

For his ears are so acute that they sting again.

For from this proceeds the passing quickness of his attention.
For by stroking of him I have found out electricity.
For I perceived God's light about him both wax and fire.
For the Electrical fire is the spiritual substance, which
    God sends from heaven to sustain the bodies both of
    man and beast.
For God has blessed him in the variety of his movements.
For, tho he cannot fly, he is an excellent clamberer.
For his motions upon the face of the earth are more than
    any other quadrupede.
For he can tread to all the measures upon the music.
For he can swim for life.
For he can creep.

This seems to me a quite wonderful poem. There's a very good and affectionate little spoof of it by another poet, Peter Reading, in his book -273.15 ('For I will consider my cat Tikka:/ For she is an atheist;' etc).

Since we're on poets, I should admit that – being an embarrassingly pretentious character – I named my own cat after the hero of the poet John Berryman's *Dream Songs*. I called my cat Henry. Then I found out she was female. Oops. So it goes.

What's she like? She is a black mog, probably mostly Burmese, a bit over two years old, with a white blaze at the throat that makes her look a tiny bit like a vicar (another category of warmly regarded but inscrutable creatures that suddenly became female). She's an indoor cat: she lives in a first-floor flat in South London, and her rare encounters with other cats, dogs, and above all chickens, have been mixed successes.

She is a mixture of gravity and waggery. She is an excellent clamberer. And, on command... well, perhaps I haven't trained her so well as Mad Dog Smart did Jeoffrey. She waggles not, nor does she spraggle. In fact, she does exactly what cats do when issued with a command: treats it with indifference. One word from me, and she does exactly what she likes.

There are certain interesting secrets that cat-owners know. One of them is that – contrary to their PR – cats are not half so co-ordinated as everyone thinks. Henry very often climbs up the folding rack on which I dry my clothes; and, equally often, loses her footing and falls down, bashing her furry bonce on every bar on the way down. She looks around, whenever this happens, to make quite sure that nobody noticed. Embarrassment is an emotion that cats, alone among quadrupeds, detectably suffer.

Another secret cat-owners know is that cats are picky, and not always in the way you'd like. I wanted to feed old Henry the sort of super-expensive pellets of Science Diet-style hand-caught vitamin-enriched organic supermodel tuna that I feel befits her position as the chief emotional interest in my tragic man-spinster life. Turns out the cat – in whom I'd reposed all my hopes of social betterment – is a chav. Offered a sliver of smoked salmon, she sniffs it, recoils from it as if in offence, and waits for it to dry out until it's hard as a twist of old denim. Then she bats it around as a toy. The only thing she really loves is Go-Cat. Which she gobbles up, only occasionally contracting minor lower-urinary-tract infections.

She stalks around me. Sometimes in the small hours of the morning I hear her call from downstairs with that uniquely plaintive and attention-getting cat-cry familiar to all who've lived with one. Even half-asleep, I suck air through my teeth as noisily as I can. There'll be a pause, a mkgnao (as James Joyce, brilliantly, transcribed it), and then the sound of bounding and galloping as she makes her way up the stairs, claws useful as ever for sharp turns on carpet. A hiatus, while she's in the air. A soft thump. And the instant she lands on my bed she starts purring.

I'll reach sleepily out, hoping to get an affectionate smear of her cheek with a knuckle. And she'll bugger, immediately, off. She'll ignore my Egyptian cotton duvet, and goose-feather pillows, and love-hungry companionship-seeking self, and curl up on the floor. This, I think, finally, is why cats are so fascinating. They don't give us unconditional love – as any horrible drooling dog, canine or human, does... rather, they give us unconditional indifference.

That's much more valuable. These creatures – however we adore them, and fuss over them, and imagine they dote on us – are profoundly alien. I look into Henry's lozenge-shaped eyes, and I have no idea at all what goes on in her head. I certainly don't flatter myself that she'd duck into a burning building to rescue me if I were on fire. In fact, I reckon, she'd bound away from the smoke, sit tight at a safe distance, and look upon her forepaws to see if they were clean. Cats are emotionally opaque, capriciously affectionate and, finally, their own thing.

That's why I love my cat to death – and why I have so loved certain similar humans – and why I am, as we cat-lovers all are, doomed. Regarding Henry.

Why I love my cat

RICKY GERVAIS

I love my cat because that's what you're meant to do. I love all animals because they are, without exception, unconditionally beautiful and perfect. I love Ollie more than other animals because she is indeed beautiful and perfect but I also know her well. She is mine. Less like a friend more like an offspring.

SURPRISE

You see, I didn't choose her like a friend; she was a gift. Jonathan Ross gave her to me on his chat show. My last cat Colin died and Jonathan as a surprise presented little Ol to me in a pink ribbon. Even the four poofs thought this was a bit gay but I was touched (not in that way) by the gift and even hugged Mr Ross as a thank you. (Footballers hug all the time.)

I didn't love her straight away, obviously. She wouldn't have been my favourite breed on paper (Tonkinese); I always thought anything with Siamese in it was a little bit 'designery'. I liked moggies. My first cat was a tabby called Paddy, as was my second called Wilf, who we got from Battersea Dogs' Home. If that didn't give it a complex, calling it Wilf surely did. Wilf was a she. As was Colin, also a rescue cat and a big fat black and white thing that used to leave its tongue out by mistake after washing.

'HUGGING'

I loved all my cats but feel I now love Ollie more. I hope I feel the same about my next cat. Because that's the way it should be. I can't imagine loving a cat more than Ollie at the moment but then I think I must have felt that way about Paddy and Colin and Wilf.

Hugging a famous fop on national television whilst holding a kitten in a ribbon was until now the gayest thing I had ever done. But I've just written an article called 'Why I love my cat'. Me and my cat live with my girlfriend, by the way.

My cat

DEBORAH MOGGACH

Fifteen years ago one of my children's friends was walking along Kilburn High Road when he saw a mail-sack lying in the gutter. Inside it, something stirred. He reached in and pulled out a kitten. He didn't know what on earth to do with it, he couldn't look after it, but then he thought of us. He put it in his pocket and brought it round to our house in Camden Town.

Not surprisingly, we called the kitten Kilburn. How anyone could have wanted to get rid of him, in such a sadistic manner, is beyond my understanding. He's a silver tabby – rather unusual colouring, almost black – and as he's grown up he has shown no signs of his traumatic start. In fact he's particularly sturdy and steady in character – an untroubled sort of chap. You'd think he would have been brutalised by such a start in life, or would be one of those needy creatures that are constantly seeking affection, but he's not bothered.

Kilburn is just friendly with everybody. In fact he's well known in the neighbourhood because he sits on the pavement watching people go by, and most of them give him a stroke. He also waits for me there when I'm out, and always seems to know when I'm returning so he can get into position on the gate-post to greet me.

I always suspect people who over-invest their pets with sensitivity, but Kilburn can behave with extraordinary empathy. I had a seven-year love affair, and when that broke up and the man moved out, Kilburn moved into my bed for several nights. He actually climbed into bed beside me, between the sheets, like a person, and kept watch on me all night. Whenever I woke, his eyes were wide open, gazing at me with a sort of sorrowful tenderness.

Enough of that, it does sound dippy. A woman anthropomorphising her cat seems so spinsterish, doesn't she? The sort of woman who makes quilts and grows spider plants. Who hoards her yogurt pots and mistrusts men. So I'll stop.

Kilburn is just a very nice companion. He specialises in bizarre sleeping positions – legs splayed, all sorts of contortions. He never catches birds, thank goodness, though he has occasionally brought in a fieldmouse for me as an unwanted present. He's far too laid-back to take any notice of the dog, a border collie, who has a rather unhinged obsession with him. However much the dog barks at him, rushes at him, tries to get his attention, Kilburn doesn't give a toss. I admire such *sang-froid*. As someone remarked, he's the epitome of cool.

We've had a very contented fifteen years together. His only drawback is a finickyness about food. I know lots of cats are like this but it doesn't stop it being annoying. The moment I discover that Kilburn actually likes something – Whiskas tuna flakes or whatever – and buy several packets, he'll suddenly decide not to eat it anymore. It's his only neurosis. What he really likes is to eat what I'm eating; he likes to share in things.

The only other annoying thing about him is that he lies on my work. Cats always do this, don't they? Whichever piece of paper you're reading, or trying to write on – that's the exact piece the cat will go to sleep on. They know it by a sort of radar. I think, like the food, it's their way of muscling in on one's life.

But most of the time, of course, they're extremely self-sufficient. That's why we like them; they have their own parallel life, separate from ours, but co-existing with it quite happily. We don't notice each other for days. It's like the least demanding of marriages, really. And, indeed, has lasted longer than mine did.

The real Mog

JUDITH KERR

We'd always wanted a cat and as soon as we owned a house and a garden, we got one. We got Mog.

The children loved her and she was remarkably tolerant of them. When our two-year-old picked her up and carried her – fondly, but upside down – she would roll her eyes at us as much as to say, 'See what I have to put up with?' But she never scratched or bit. She rarely miaowed, perhaps because of the constant noise from the children, and so she had to rely on visual effects to make her wishes known.

When she thought it was time for her supper and we were watching television, she would sit on the set and hang her tail down over the screen. When she wanted to come in from the garden – refusing on principle to use her cat flap – she would sit on the window box outside the kitchen and I'd look up from the sink to see this terrible face staring in at me. After a while we stopped planting flowers in that window box because they always got squashed.

Her hunting expeditions were often a disappointment. Her great ambition was to catch a squirrel, and she'd pursue one up to the very top of the huge oak tree across the road, whereupon the squirrel would leap over to the next tree and leave her stranded and having to clamber down sixty feet in a very humiliating manner.

She also always hoped to catch one of the sparrows on the roof, but they were too cunning for her. They would tease her by fluttering just out of her reach until one day, when she leapt to grab one, she accidentally leapt right off the roof. My husband happened to be looking out of the window and he suddenly saw a furry shape shooting past. We all rushed downstairs. We were sure she'd been killed, but she just picked herself up and walked a little stiffly to the boiler, where she sat for a long time looking very thoughtful.

She was so much part of our lives that when I started doing picture books I thought I would make one about her, putting in all the things she did as well as all the things the children and my husband made up about her. Mog was immediately very interested in this. She would come up to the room where I worked at the top of the house and sit on my lap, and as I drew and painted the pictures she would watch the paintbrush, and sometimes she would nudge it very gently with her nose.

As more Mog books followed it became a regular practice. But the odd thing is that she only did it when I was working on a book about her. I also wrote and illustrated other books, but when I was working on those she kept away.

She lived to be eighteen and in the last years her hind legs tended to give way and she hardly moved from her place by the boiler in the kitchen. By then there had been quite a few Mog books, and the children used to say what a pity it was that she didn't know she was famous. However, when the BBC suggested making a short film about her we first said no because we thought it might upset her. But they promised to be very careful, so in the end we agreed to let them try.

We needn't have worried. As soon as the camera crew arrived Mog seemed to understand that this was her chance to be a star. She took direction. She did the business with the cat flap. She made her terrible face on the window box. She did everything they asked her. We couldn't believe it. But, as she seemed happy, we wondered whether she might even sit on my lap while I worked – something she hadn't done for years because, with her fragile hind legs, she could no longer climb the many stairs to my workroom. So I carried her up the two flights and she became very excited at seeing the top floor again. And when I got out my paints and brushes she sat on my lap and watched what I was doing and after a while she nudged the paintbrush with her nose. They got it all on film and she finished off her performance with a full minute's purr into the microphone for the soundman.

Finally I carried her back downstairs and put her in her basket. But much later that evening, long after the camera crew had gone home, I went up to the top of the house to fetch something, and there was Mog. Goodness knows how she managed the stairs but she must have wanted to take one more look at her past. She walked very slowly across the landing into my workroom and then into my husband's workroom, and she looked very carefully at all the things – at the desks and the typewriters and the papers and the paints and at the chairs she used to lie in and the windows she used to climb out of – and when she had seen everything she lay down on the floor, and I carried her back down the stairs to her basket and she purred and went to sleep.

That was one of the last things she did. She died soon afterwards. But she died knowing that she was famous.

THE TRUTH ABOUT CATS

Based on rigorous observations made as cats go about their strange and unintelligable activities

fig 1 - Staring blankly into thin air.

NOTHING

Thousands of years of natural selection have resulted in these 3

Laws of Cat Behaviour:

ii – When offered a finger or a pencil, a cat will touch it with its nose.

i – A cat will always sit on a piece of paper no matter how small.

a:

b:

comfy...

iii – Cats will sit in a box for no reason whatsoever.

FINGER

PENCIL

I have a good reason for doing this.

?

MOSES

MAGGIE O'FARRELL

My sister arrived at my flat one night with a zealous gleam in her eye. 'I've found you something,' she said. 'What?' I said. I think I was attempting to coax my son on to the potty at the time and was only half-listening. 'The perfect cat,' she replied. She is a vet and works one day a week at a cat rescue centre. The embodiment of feline perfection was nine months old, she said, sweet natured, would be good with children, was black with white feet. Oh, and he'd been a persistent giardia sufferer (an gastro-intestinal parasite) and had been in solitary confinement since birth.

I straightened up from the potty training. 'No,' I said, 'no way.' She is forever trying to foist cats with various unappealing afflictions on to me. Only the week before I'd had to be very firm about a Persian with alopecia. The last thing I needed was an animal with social problems and a history of infectious diseases. It was out of the question.

Moses arrived roughly twenty-four hours later, with more luggage than a starlet: a blanket, a collapsible play-tunnel, several toy mice, a collar and a litter tray the size of a small car. We peered into the dark interior of the carrying case; I could make out a white blaze down the nose, like a horse's, and two eyes that flashed with abject terror.

What must it be like to spend your life in solitary confinement and then be transported to a household of people desperate to see you, to play with you, to stroke you? Because of the highly infectious nature of the giardia he'd been born with, he'd never seen another cat, not even his own mother. He'd spent his entire life in a concrete cage. The only people he'd ever seen were my sister, fleetingly, and his carer, Wendy, who would come in at the end of her day to play with him.

He didn't come out for two days and when he did the thing that petrified him was not the vacuum or a visiting dog or even an over-keen toddler. It was the ceiling. One glance upwards was enough to send him haring back to the safety of his red case. After all that time in an enclosed cell, the towering height of the room was too much for him.

After he'd got over his reverse vertigo, he became the most intensely curious creature I've ever come across. Everything interested him; nothing was too banal or mundane. The Velcro on the sofa, the cooker dials, the fluff under the wardrobe, the ignition on the gas fire, coat zips, cardigan buttons, door handles, a patch on my son's knee, an Elastoplast worn by my husband. The house was a sensory overload for him and everything must be investigated.

Things got tricky when he discovered the fascination of a cursor on a computer screen and, better still, words unscrolling across a document. He wanted to sit in front of the screen, head cocked, as I worked. I lifted him down but, as soon as I resumed typing, he was back. I removed him again; he came back. Eventually I had to put him outside and he reappeared at the window, glaring at the computer screen and me.

He still has the habit of vanishing for hours at a stretch, only to reappear mysteriously coated with dust. He likes to explore each and every odd corner, unusually small space, tiny crack in the fabric of the house. It's like living with an extremely small escapologist. I'll come upon him wedged inside an open desk drawer, crouched high up on the

pelmet. Sometimes there will be a scrabbling noise and Moses will tumble down the chimney, landing with a thud in the grate. I once had to dismantle the piano, after hearing piteous miaowing from inside.

We are having building work done at the moment — kitchen cupboards pulled off the walls, floorboards ripped up. Moses is tense, wired, stalking the house like a particularly rigorous foreman. I have become neurotic about him getting trapped under the floor. 'We haven't seen him,' the builders assure me as they go to replace the boards. 'He's not under there.' But I'm certain that he will be and I crouch beside the hole, calling his name, rattling the cat biscuits. He invariably re-emerges, when it suits him, when he's finished his surveillance, grey with dust, a preoccupied yet satisfied look in his eye. Another part of the house ticked off, another unknown territory mapped out in his head.

Digging up the cat

AUDREY NIFFENEGGER

It's a lovely Sunday afternoon in late October, just after lunch, when Dad and I decide it is time to dig up my cat. We've been meaning to do it for a while, but other chores had always seemed more pressing, and if we don't do it now the ground is going to freeze again and we'll have to wait till spring.

'What are you guys up to?' Mom asks, seeing us gathering the shovels and the rubber gloves and the wheelbarrow.

'Digging up Beardsley,' I tell her.

'Oh. Be sure to put the rose bush back when you're done.'

'K.'

Beardsley has been in the ground for almost exactly seven years. We had buried him at dusk on an October day that was warmer and softer than this one. We put him in a pine box I had painted electric blue. It was sad; Beardsley had dropped dead at the age of six, for no good reason that I could see. Now we are digging him up.

Dad hands me a trowel. 'Just move those plants so your Mom doesn't get excited,' he says. I carefully dig up the rose and a strange spiky ground-cover sort of plant. Then we start to dig. The earth is damp and clay heavy. It clings to the shovels. We fill the wheelbarrow.

'How far was it?' Dad asks.

'Just a couple of feet down,' I say. We get down to the box, find the edges of it, dig around it, ease it up, lift it out and lay it on the grass. It's covered with dirt and one side of the box has caved in a bit. I get soapy water and a rag and wipe off the box.

We are digging up my cat because his sister, Jane, has died. Actually, Jane died last December. Since the ground was frozen under two feet of snow, I wrapped Jane carefully in plastic and placed her gently in my freezer, where she has resided ever since. Whenever I open the freezer to get some orange juice or a waffle I greet her: 'Hi, Jane.' Sometimes I tell her about current events, or the weather. Mostly I just like knowing she's there. But other people find it strange that there's a cat in my freezer. 'Are you going to eat it?' asked a perplexed guest. 'No, I'm going to bury her when the ground thaws.' He glanced out the window at my baking July backyard, and looked alarmed.

We are digging up my cat because my parents are thinking of selling their house, my childhood home, and my mother feels it would be too weird to leave a box full of dead cat in the garden. So, just as I've taken my share of the Christmas ornaments (although I never put up a tree and I'm not even Catholic anymore) and have hauled my old books and toys from their attic to mine (even though I have no children), I am moving my dead cat to my own garden. R.I.P.

Dad has filled up the hole and comes over to where I'm kneeling on the lawn next to the box. 'Are you going to open it?' he asks.

'I guess. I mean, I have to, if I'm putting Jane in there.'

He continues to stand there. I open the box.

Inside is a beautiful, delicate cat skull, brown and nestled in brown sludge amidst bones of many intricate shapes. A jigsaw puzzle that was a cat. Tiny white maggots busy themselves over burst parchment skin fragments. I close the lid.

'There's plenty of room in there,' Dad says cheerfully. 'You could put ten cats in there, if you did it at long enough intervals.' Ten cats at seven-year intervals equals seventy years' worth of cats. That should be enough. That ought to cover it.

Back at my house, I leave the box in the garden. I open the back door and take off my boots, open the freezer and carefully remove Jane from her niche among the ice cubes and chicken breasts. I set her on the kitchen counter, cut off the plastic with scissors, unwrap her. She's frozen into an uncomfortable position, sort of rectangular. I decide to thaw her before I put her in the box. I touch her grey fur. She is hard as a rock.

Later, Jane is pliable and I have dug a hole near the grape arbour. I wrap her in a piece of cotton fabric, carry her outside, and lay her in the grass. The sun is going down; it's getting cold. I remove the plastic from the blue box, and open the lid. I pick Beardsley's little skull out of the sludge, holding it carefully so the jawbone doesn't detach. I'm grateful that eyes decay before bone. I replace his skull in a corner of the box and place Jane next to the skull. She is heavy, like a fur-covered IV bag of blood. 'Goodbye,' I tell her. I will miss seeing her in the freezer.

As I shovel earth over the cats I have a sense of déjà vu. Perhaps it's a presentiment of all the cats to come, all the things and people I will lose. In the garden everything is brown and the grape leaves rattle above my head as I shovel.

That evening I call home to tell Dad about it, that feeling I'm having trouble putting a name to.

'You okay?' he asks.

'Yeah. I'm okay,' I say. After a while, it will be true.

Paddy

AND Buster

LYNNE TRUSS

In the summer of 1986, I acquired two tiny kittens. One kitten was obtained in a conventional way through a friend at work; the other – a female with slightly mad tortoiseshell markings – was found on a traffic island in London's Clerkenwell Road.

A lot has happened in my life since 1986. In those far-off days I was thin, had quite good dress-sense, and was just about to start a lovely job at the BBC's *Listener* magazine that I assumed would be mine for life. But things didn't turn out that way. *The Listener* folded in 1991. Since then, I've been through two long-term relationships, moved house a couple of times, had four or five different jobs, adopted the contact lens and then reverted to specs, published nine books, flirted with financial ruin, survived the shocking premature deaths of three close family members, become an international heroine to pedants, and experimented with several styles of haircut.

Only one thing of any significance remained the same for all that time: the presence of my two cats. And now, suddenly, my two cats are reduced to one and the survivor is thin and wobbly. Perhaps I shouldn't be surprised by how I'm feeling. Loving animals is all tied up with dreading their loss. I've dreaded the loss of Paddy for twenty years. Now that I don't have to worry about her any more, I feel curiously at peace.

On the morning of 18 December, I came downstairs and found Paddy lying oddly on her side, legs outstretched. I called her and she didn't move. I approached and she didn't notice. I reached to stroke her, and she was cold. It was as if someone had come along in the night and replaced her with a stuffed animal. And while I stroked her and cried, I knew that she had actually done a brilliant thing. She had topped off a splendid life with a splendid death and, at the same time as I felt such sadness, I truly admired and loved her for it.

Paddy was the kitten found on the traffic island. No one knew how she got herself there, of course, although, in my more far-fetched moments, I have pictured her as an exotic princess kitten bravely escaping from desperadoes heading east to Limehouse, having snatched her from somewhere fashionable in West London. ('She got away? In Clerkenwell Road? You idiots!') Paddy turned out to have magnificent fur and excellent teeth, which surely confirmed her high-birth origins. If there was ever a cat suited to purple velvet with gold frogging, it was Pad.

But back in the realm of reality, she was a true party girl, in contrast to my other cat, who simply disapproves of fun. While Paddy would chase around the light from a torch beam in figures of eight, Buster would not only assume a grave expression, but sometimes actually block her path. Tie a bit of paper to some string and Paddy would pat it and play, while

Buster would catch it, hold it tight, and then, if possible, saw through the string with his incisors to put an emphatic end to such foolishness. These two cats were not bosom friends, as you can imagine. Paddy was the Diana Dors of the cat world; Buster is its Citizen Robespierre.

People had to see this to believe it, but Paddy would actually lie happily in a plastic shopping basket while I swung it back and forth, higher and higher until it was horizontal to horizontal. Not many cats enjoy fairground thrills, but she did. In fact, sometimes I'd be racing for a train, coat on, almost at the front door, and I'd find she'd hopped into the basket with an unmistakable air of expectation. 'But I'm late, Pad!' I'd protest. 'Miaow,' she'd say loudly. And that was that. I'd put down my bag, take off my coat and get right down to the swinging.

It wasn't in the plan that Paddy should go first. She seemed perfectly well, and it was obvious to everyone that she would survive Buster. A dear friend in America sent me a poetic elegy, based on Tennyson's *In Memoriam* and called it *In Miaowiam*, which was so perfectly funny and sad it broke my heart. I am thinking of reading it aloud, one day soon, on a certain significant traffic island in the middle of Clerkenwell Road.

✻ TIGER ROSE

CATHERINE TATE

We decided to get a cat when my little girl asked for a dog. Although I've never been much of an animal person I was keen for her to have one because I think it's nice for children to grow up with a pet. A dog, however, was too much of a commitment – walking it three times a day and all that business of scooping up its poo in a plastic bag is not for me. You might as well have another child. So we decided on a cat, a nice fluffy, independent, low-maintenance cat.

I must confess to being a bit cat phobic in the past. Their little cat heads and stretchy spines used to really creep me out but I was now willing to fight my urge to retch whenever one came near for the sake of my four-year-old, who had her heart set on a girl kitten she could name Rose. Plus they take care of their own poo. We went to the Battersea Cats' and Dogs' Home, had the interview where you take a test to see how clued up you are on all things feline, and passed, but there was nothing suitable so we went home and waited for a phone call. It came quicker than I'd expected.

'We've had some kittens come in,' The Lady From Battersea said (hereafter referred to as TLFB). 'Oh my God, that's brilliant news,' I replied, getting all excited and nervous like a prospective adoptive parent. We'd bought all the equipment and were all geared up for a little furry addition to the family. The phone call went like this.

TLFB: *We've had a beautiful smoky grey kitten come in.*

ME: *Fantastic.*

TLFB: *Yes, it's really unusual to get this colour and he's very sweet natured.*

ME: *Perfect.*

TLFB: *There's a little problem though.*

ME: *Oh?*

TLFB: *He's got a prolapsed rectum.*

ME: (Pause) *What does that mean?*

TLFB: *It means the inner layers of the rectum push out through the anus.*

ME: *What does that mean?*

TLFB: *It means his rectum sometimes hangs out of his bottom and you'll have to gently push it back in.*

ME: (Feeling a bit sick) *Right.*

TLFB: *How do you think you'd cope with that?*

ME: *Not very well to be honest.* (Pause) *Sorry.*

It was going to be challenging enough for me to have an animal in the house in the first place. Having one that dragged its rectum along the floor was too big an ask. Or indeed arse. We agreed that the beautiful smoky kitten should go to someone a little more experienced in the art of cat handling. A couple of days later she rang again.

TLFB: *I've got another one.*

ME: *Great.*

TLFB: *There's just one thing.*

ME: (Thinking, you've got to be joking. What's the matter with this one? Is it blind?) *Oh?*

TLFB: *I'm not sure how you'll feel about this…*

ME: (Now convinced it's blind) *OK?*

TLFB: *Some people just won't consider them.*

ME: *Is it blind?*

TLFB: (Shocked) *No. It's ginger.*

ME: (Equally shocked) *Pardon?*

TLFB: *It's ginger.*

ME: *Why is that a problem?*

TLFB: *Well, some people just don't want them.*

I am outraged. Being myself a fully paid-up member of the ginger club, I can't believe what I'm hearing. The discrimination against my race has filtered down and now even ginger animals are being victimised. She said it's because their colouring is so common that some people prefer not to take them. But I know the real reason is that in their hearts people secretly think that ginger cats, like ginger people, smell of wee.

It was a done deal. This was the kitten for us and we drove to Battersea in a state of nervous excitement. I'd not told my daughter that it was a tom cat we were on our way to get because she was still adamant that she only wanted a girl cat called Rose ('Like Billie Piper in *Dr Who*,' she would remind us frequently). We arrived to find the most adorable little kitten in the world waiting for us and fell in love with him instantly. When I tentatively told my child that 'Rose' was in fact a boy, adding hopefully, 'But we don't mind do we because he's so gorgeous?', she went ballistic, sobbing and protesting at TLFB. So great was her distress that to this day she still calls him her. To be honest, she still calls him Rose.

I've tried to butch his name up a little by suggesting we call him Tiger Rose but she's not convinced. All I know is, boy or girl this wonderful little animal has enhanced our lives in a way I could not have imagined. I surprise myself with how much I love him and how much I miss him when I don't see him. I might as well have had another child. And he only smells very faintly of wee.

Summer and Spot

ZOE WILLIAMS

The night after C and I first got it on, I called him to see if he wanted to come over again. It wasn't what you'd call appropriate. I had a table full of people and I was as drunk as a sock. It would all have been quite sudden, and open to misinterpretation. It's not, put it this way, how they tell you to go about dating in *The Rules*. Anyway, he said no. He'd been out the whole night before (well, I knew that). And he had cat-guilt.

I had honestly never heard anything so ludicrous in my life. Dog-guilt, I understand. If I'd left my dog on his own for a whole night, I'd… well, I don't know what I'd do because that would never happen. But cats, for god's sake, how do you feel guilty about a cat? You leave it some food, you up off, it fends for itself. It runs out of food; it finds some more. It gets lonely; ten seconds later it finds a new home. It's like feeling guilty for cheating on Casanova. So I figured this was a lame but nevertheless thoughtful excuse for his not being all that into me, and even though I was naturally surprised, let's call me blankly astonished, by this turn of events (I was drunk, remember. I was on top of the world! I thought I was He-Man, only more feminine!), I was also thirty, and not eighteen, so I didn't take it too much to heart.

That is not how it turned out. It was the worst misreading of a human heart I'd made since, well, all those other hearts I've misread and never found out about. I don't want to tempt fate by going on about how into me he turned out to be, but he did at least turn out to be, you know, into me enough. He just happened to be really serious about his cat.

Summer has a lovely nature, a fine-looking white-and-pastel coat, and she is the most explosively ugly creature you have ever seen. Photographs don't do her justice. Her chin points inwards, back towards her body. The expression on her face is a kind of stoic bafflement. 'How come I look like this?' I think of her wondering. 'Why don't I look like all those other cats?' People ask questions like 'was she born like that, or did something happen to her?' Spot, conversely, is so physically perfect (apart from his lack of balls, but I only have myself and the vet to blame) that sometimes I'm embarrassed to stand next to him. I feel like Woody Allen next to Mia Farrow.

That information is irrelevant, and it certainly isn't how I came to think we'd end up with a dog, and not a cat. The dog is large and can be a savage kind of beauty. He bit my mother. He bit my uncle at my dad's funeral. When he sees my sister's cat, his whole hindquarters shake with excitement, like he's standing on an electrocuted pad. Even though he's been retrained to his core since the human incidents, he is not a dog you'd want to rehome; the only alternative to keeping him would be to have him put down, which is of course out of the question. Summer, on the other hand, could be rehomed anywhere. She has an adorable temperament. She'd be a lovely addition to any household, especially one full of blind people.

As we came closer to moving in together, C kept saying, 'I'd never forgive myself if we didn't at least try to introduce them', and I'd nod, and think 'yeah, and she'll see him, and immediately run away, but so long as he doesn't kill her first, our relationship will probably survive.' I brought him a leaflet about introducing dogs to cats from Dogs Trust, but it was underpinned by my thinking he was admirably loyal, a stayer, a slogger and a slugger; he had all the qualities I wanted in a life-partner, but he was also a total idiot. You should have heard my mother on the subject (she hates Spot). 'C is a total idiot,' she would say, loud and often. It transpires that he knew I agreed with her (and I think I've got such a poker face), but he kept his counsel (you will forgive my fairytale tone).

The week we moved in to the house we'd bought together, me and Spot went away, ostensibly to let Summer get used to her new home, but really because I was trying to be as accommodating as possible, to offset the raging bestiality of my pet. We came back; Summer was in the kitchen, and I came downstairs with Spot on the lead, as per our leaflet. His haunches started to shake. I waited for Summer to scarper, but she looked at C and closed her eyes. It was extraordinary. About three times, Spot had a shot at chasing her when he thought I wasn't looking, and she swiped him. I've got to stress again the differential in their sizes and strength – he is a staffie crossed with a ridgeback. And she hit him on the nose. For about three weeks, he had a pink patch that wouldn't heal. I guess because he kept having a sniff, and she kept hitting him.

And that was that. Under his sixty-six pounds of solid muscle, like many bullies, Spot was a coward and soon just started leaving her alone. I would be lying if I said I loved them both the same. But that is history, and the fact that he's, like, a dog. Summer has all my respect, all my admiration, and, under her demure manners, the bollocks of a matador.

HOW TO UNDERSTAND WHAT
YOUR CAT IS SAYING

CELIA HADDON

Your cat has probably worked out how to ask for food and also how to get you to open a door for it. Some cats even let their owners know when it is time (in the cat's opinion) for bed. A surprising number have mastered the tricky business of waking up their owners for a regular 5 a.m. snack.

All this and they don't even use words! You, for your part, probably know when your feline friend is feeling miserable. You can recognise an ill cat. You know when your cat is particularly enjoying its meal. You know when you have irritated it.

Yet when it comes to communication, our two species are using foreign languages with each other. We humans primarily use complicated series of vocal sounds that form words. Tone and pitch of voice vary the meaning. We also use body language as a form of expression.

The communication by scent that is common among animals is, of course, fairly minimal among us. We can learn very little by giving another human being a good sniff, as we have a poor sense of smell.

Cats, on the other hand, communicate (at least to humans) primarily by means of body language. Secondarily, they use scent and tactile contact. And thirdly, they use vocal noises. Scent messages from a cat to a human are often ignored or misunderstood. As well as keener hearing and a better sense of smell, cats have a tactile sense organ: their whiskers. These are used more to receive information that to send it.

The better you understand cat talk, the more you will understand your cat.

How to read your cat's body language

When humans use body language to convey messages, the main area of communication is the face, with its smiles, frowns and tears. Dogs also use facial language; they can wrinkle their brows, smile, hang their tongues out, and their facial expression transmits mood messages recognisable to humans. Cat faces are relatively immobile and are difficult for humans to read correctly. But there are some clear signs.

Understanding eye messages In cat society, it is not polite to stare. A cat that wishes to avoid aggression will avoid eye contact, often by turning its face to one side. Blinking (or narrowed eyes) is another way cats show politeness.

Eye-to-eye confrontation between two cats shows potential aggression. A cat that retreats with a fixed stare is telling an enemy that, if cornered, it will fight. For this reason, humans should take off spectacles if dealing with a frightened cat. Blinking or looking away is also reassuring.

The cat's fear of glaring eyes may also partly account for the way it goes towards people who dislike cats, as those people tend to make eye contact with them. Intense watching, but not eye-to-eye staring, is also part of the predatory sequence, and may precede a play pounce on another cat.

Understanding tail messages The tail position of a cat going about its business is horizontal or slightly lowered. There is also a tail-up greeting, where a friendly cat comes towards its companion (human or other friendly cat) with its tail held high, often with a slight curve forwards at the very tip. This tail-up greeting is not found in wild cats and may have developed during domestication.

Tail-up is also used during body rubbing (which also has a scent message) as the cat weaves itself in and around human feet. Normally, a cat rubbing round its human's legs is trying to get attention. A forward tail tip curve is friendly, but there is also a hostile hello in which the bottom half of the tail is raised outwards, but the main part of the tail is curved down. Before a fight, a hostile cat will pull its tail down to get out of the way. A crouching terrified cat has its tail tucked right out of sight. No cat wants to risk damage to its tail.

A cat that is twitching or lashing its tail is usually considering attack. Tail twitching or lashing usually occurs before the pounce, during the cat's hunting stalk. It also occurs when a cat is contemplating an attack on another cat or a human.

Finally, the tail plays a part in feline sexual signals. A female cat on heat will crouch with its backside raised towards the male, its tail held on one side. Pet cats sometimes do a flirty version of this to their humans. They present their backsides, but with the tail up in the friendly greeting posture rather than held aside in the sexual come-on signal.

Understanding claw and paw messages Cats keep their claws sheathed and walk on their toes. Claws come out to help run up trees or attack. They are used as a weapon during the predatory pounce. A cat with its paw slightly lifted is ready to cuff you! A human with a hand outstretched may look threatening to a cat.

Using cat language

The key to understanding any new foreign language is experience. An inexperienced cat, which is trying to read us, will be better at reading our body language than our vocal words. Yet an experienced cat can understand some of our words – such as the word 'vet'.

The more experience a cat gains around humans, the more words it knows and the more it uses its voice to get through to us.

Talking to your cat

If you want to communicate better with your cat, you can use some of its own signals. With a frightened cat, be careful to give it just sideways glances, not a glare. You can try to become lower than the cat. Let it get up higher onto a table or shelf, while you go down to ground level, flat on your tummy.

Inexperienced humans often spend hours of effort in trying to understand a cat's vocal calls, when it would be better to concentrate on its body language. You have probably learned some of this language already, even if you don't know you have done so. Careful attention to its ears and gestures will give further information.

Finally, you can use scent to make your cat feel secure. By petting it, you are putting the scent from your hands upon your cat's body and taking onto your hand its own body scent, thus mixing the two scents in a message of friendship. This action reassures and calms the cat.

Touch and smell points

Grooming Cats who are friendly groom each other, and some cats groom humans. This is because saliva spreads scent, too.

Rubbing to mix scents This spreads a scent from the cat's skin glands. Cats rub with their chins, their cheeks, their foreheads, flanks and tails. They rub other cats and humans, mixing their scent with others.

Rubbing to mark territory Cats rub specific marking points in their territory – against shrubs, walls, doorways and large plants.

Scratching The scent glands between a cat's toes leave a smell on the scratched area. Scratching is also a visual signal.

Spraying Entire tom cats spray, but so, at times, do neutered males and females. The cat stands at full height, arches its back, and squirts a jet of urine. The body posture shows that this is territorial marking.

Middening The cat uses faeces to send a message as well as to mark territory. The faeces are left uncovered as a visual as well as a scent signal. Faeces are often left along walkways at the edge of territory.

Squat marking Just to confuse their humans, cats will occasionally mark territory by urinating when squatting. This marking can only be distinguished from ordinary urination by its location. It is said that the urine smells are more pungent than ordinary urine.

Talking points

Chirrup This is a little chirrup or trill used as a greeting between cats and their kittens, sometimes to humans.

Purr Used when nursing kittens or as a response to tactile contact. It can be switched on by the physical nearness of familiar humans or by familiar pleasant places. Some cats purr almost silently, creating more of a vibration than a sound.

Meow An attention-seeking noise which varies in length. The meaning varies with context. Some cats are almost silent. Older cats meow more than younger ones – probably because they know their humans take more notice of sound than body language. Orientals use long meows frequently.

Growl A warning sign of aggression. Cats that growl are seriously angry and may bite!

Yowl On a rising note, a warning sound.

Hiss A defensive sound, meaning 'back off'.

Spit A more violently defensive sound.

Chatter This is an involuntary excited predatory noise, made when a cat is watching prey but cannot get at it.

Caterwauling & sexual calls Neutered and spayed cats don't need or use them – for obvious reasons.

25 ways to make your cat adore you

INGRID NEWKIRK

1. Your cat must have a comfy place to sit and look out. While outwardly cats appear aloof, just below the surface they are like that nosey neighbour in *Bewitched*. Provided with a view, your cat will have something to distract her from resenting your absence. Ordinary windowsills are usually too small to accommodate even svelte feline bottoms. A cat likes to survey her domain while stretching or lounging and does not like to be seen wobbling. Try dragging a piece of furniture over to the window and firmly attach a cushion to it. Cats love to

sunbathe so make it an east- or west-facing cat seat, if you can. Oh, and if Tiddles is occupying your favourite comfy chair, you wouldn't move her, would you?

2. Litter tray alert: a truly happy cat never has to wrinkle his nose when using his litter tray. The entire contents should be dumped daily, and the tray swilled with vinegar, washed with soap, then rinsed and dried. Never use a pine-based cleaner; it can be toxic. You don't need to use masses of litter – just enough to cover the base of the tray – and keep the tray away from the place where he eats. In multi-cat households, there should be no less than one tray per two cats.

3. Cats love small, dark spaces. Avoid folding beds and rocking chairs, and be careful when closing drawers: kitty could be squashed or trapped. Always check your washing machine and dryer before turning them on.

4. Play with your cat. Cats are thoughtful, clever and innovative. Without stimulation they become bored and resentful. Try scrunching up bits of tinfoil and tossing them across the room. Or pinecones. The People for the Ethical Treatment of Animals (PETA) office cats enjoy retrieving plastic lizards, which, believe it or not, they recognise as lizards, often chewing off their tails and dragging them round in their mouths looking proud.

5. A sure bet for a happy cat is catnip. Buy catnip seeds and grow it in the garden or a window box. Then stuff the leaves in a square of cotton gauze. Or put some catnip in the toe of an old sock, knot, and throw. Most cats will roll on their backs and gaze dreamily into space.

6. Always bring home a present for your cat. They love feathers, seaweed or a leaf. A few feathers tied together make for a super game of pounce.

7. Buy a cat tunnel (a washable, fleece-covered, crinkly tube that can be collapsed for storage) or a machine-washable, crawl-in bag: both wonderful ways to excite cat curiosity.

8. Look after your cat's teeth. Apparently, many cats over four years old have periodontal disease. This is because we feed our cats mush, so gums are vulnerable to infection and teeth to decay. If your cat is still a kitten, start her tooth-care regime early. Rub your finger along her teeth and gums, using a little garlicky water. As she grows, use a bumpy plastic finger guard (from your vet), graduating to a soft toothbrush with a tiny amount of special cat toothpaste. Make sure your cat's teeth are examined at least once a year and, should she have to go under general anaesthetic, seize the chance to have her teeth cleaned.

9. Never have your cat de-clawed. De-clawing is like shell shock to a cat, and creates problems while walking because cats actually walk on their toes rather than the balls of their feet. Cats also use their claws to mark territory, to keep their balance, to play. If your cat scratches your furniture, get thee to a wood or a beach, and bring home a nice stump. If you can get a chunk of tree about 1 metre (3 feet) tall, kitty will be able to stretch his claws on it nicely and then sit atop it afterwards; sprinkle it with catnip, and hang toys from the top. To deter a cat from the couch, spray it with a few drops of perfume. Or cover off-limits furniture with something slippery, such as paper. If left on for a while, your cat will move on. Four-year-old Jasmine and Ariel have persuaded their people to staple carpet off-cuts onto the wall near the door jambs, starting at about 16 centimetres (6 inches) off the floor. This allows a good stretch and scratch while keeping an eye on two rooms at once. And don't worry about your cat scratching a child. Cats are generally careful around children, recognising them as vulnerable and part of the family, and will sheath their claws.

10. Unless major surgery is required, never leave kitty at the vet, no matter how nice everyone is. Your cat depends on you to guard her against evil goings on.

11. Watch out for parasites. Worms and fleas besiege cats, and make their lives miserable. If you see any symptoms of worms, such as diarrhoea, blood or mucus in the stool, bloating, a sensitive stomach, pale gums or a dry coat, act immediately. But you should worm your cat every six months, symptoms or no. In the case of fleas, you need to attack the infestation in the home, their bedding and the cat. Use a good flea shampoo on carpets, and do not let the vacuum bag sit around, even for a moment. Put all cat bedding in a hot wash, and do it twice. And remember, the active ingredient in most commercial flea products is nerve gas. At PETA, we obtained a video of a tiny kitten in a lab cage, crying and experiencing racking convulsions in a flea shampoo test. Using too much of a product, using it too often, or using more than one product (say, collar, dip and powder) can be dangerous. So, if you decide on chemical warfare for the cat, be cautious. Young and elderly cats are especially susceptible. I would recommend soap and water, or a rinse made with one sliced lemon and about 550ml (1 pint) of hot water, steeped overnight. The next day, sponge the solution over the cat's skin and let it dry. Gentle herbal shampoos can also be effective. When shampooing, use warm water and begin with a ring of lather around the cat's neck so the fleas cannot climb onto his face. And make sure your cat's skin is healthy (a dry, flaky skin attracts fleas) by adding fresh, raw foods such as sliced carrots and broccoli and a few drops of evening primrose or flaxseed oil to his food. Aloe vera can also be used to quiet hot, itchy skin, and is harmless if licked off.

 Two cats are better than one. Anyone who has shared a bed with a cat knows that cats subscribe to the theory that too much uninterrupted sleep is bad for your health. When you have two cats and one stands on your windpipe in the middle of the night demanding you get up and play Where's the Mouse?, they will have each other. You can escort them into the living room, close the door, and go back to bed. Two cats make sense. The more satisfied and happy your cat, the less cranky and neurotic she will be. The main worry is that your cat in residence will have a hissy-fit when the newcomer arrives. Cats are not known for their magnanimity. But even the most theatrical episodes of jealousy fade. Where to get kitty number two? Rescue a cat. And if you ever find yourself starting from zero in the future, take two cats or kittens from the same family.

 Take any new family member to the vet whatever his origin to have everything checked out and make sure he is up to date with vaccinations. Set aside a room in which to treat the newcomer for anything that ails him and to allow a couple of days' peace. Make the initial introduction after a big meal, when kitties are inclined to want a good sleep. Give kitty number two the opportunity to escape the wrath of kitty number one by hiding. Then just sit there, and ignore them. If things get too tense, bring out the tinfoil balls. Reassure kitty one with lots of cooing and stroking. From the start, use as many food- and water-bowls as you have cats. With multiple bowls, you avoid unseemly spats and preserve everyone's dignity. Always place them far apart.

 Female cats should be neutered at between five and a half and six months, male cats castrated at about ten months, but they can both be 'done' sooner. If you let an uncastrated male outside, he is guaranteed to get ugly, painful abscessed ears and suffer other battle wounds that will require a vet's attention, not to mention feline Aids, for which there is no cure. Insist on collecting your cat as soon as possible after surgery, and always ask your vet for painkillers. Set aside a clean bed topped with a clean sheet in a quiet room (but not the bathroom), and make sure there are no opportunities to pole vault onto tall cabinets and separate the stitches. Place fresh cat litter and water within reach, and make sure she or he starts eating and drinking. If your cat is female, allow seven to ten days for recovery. Over the next few weeks, seize the opportunity, such as when your cat has a leg pointed at the ceiling, to take discreet peeks at the surgical site, making sure all is well.

15. Ease the travelling blues. Cats hate journeys. So don't parade about with the carrier in hand; subtlety and speed are called for. Prepare in advance, if possible, checking the carrier has a secure lock and the bottom is comfy. Try to act as if nothing is up. Once you pick the cat up, make sure you don't have far to go to the carrier. Back Tiddles into the carrier gently, talking to her, and slip a treat in through the bars. Cover the carrier with a towel, and carry it carefully. When you are in the car, put the radio on for soft background noise and talk to your cat soothingly as you travel.

16. If you go on holiday, do not put your cat in a cattery or rely on a colleague or neighbour, but hire a cat sitter who has been personally recommended to you. Meet the sitter in advance, and prepare a contract for him or her to sign. Make sure the sitter contacts you each day to let you know how your cat is. Leave phone numbers of your most cat-aware friend or relative, and that of your vet. Leave water in bowls in many rooms of the house in case your sitter is struck by lightning. Worry! This can help you think of other precautions.

17. Be prepared just in case your cat goes walkabout. Take a good picture now, and make sure he is always well dressed, i.e., with a readable, current tag on a safety collar, and a microchip. If it happens, strip search the neighbourhood. Use a torch at night; call your cat's name and then listen for a faint miaow. Make copies of his photo and glue it on every Lost and Found notice board you can find in local vets' surgeries and shelters. Stick up large posters all over your neighbourhood. Run ads in the local papers, offering a reward, and put a notice on the web, too. Make sure there's a clear message on your answer phone. Never, ever give up looking.

18. Study your cat's body language. Cats communicate a lot with their eyes. Their pupils dilate when they are angry or on the attack, and cats smile at us by squinting. Your cat will slowly, almost, but usually not quite, close her eyes and reopen them while looking at you. You can return the sentiment by squinting back. If a cat closes her eyes for more than a split second, that is absolute trust. Annoyance is commonly expressed in joint eye and tail action. Cats who miss their mums will knead you, and that's a high compliment indeed. Your cat sends messages by stretching and yawning. She is content if she throws back her head, bends her spine, extends her legs and unwinds with a yawn. Sad cats never roll on their backs. Cats also stretch to show off.

19. Learn the meaning of the tail. There are few sights more pleasing than kitty walking towards you with a big question mark tail, which means he is happy. Slow thumping of the tail is a warning. Fast swishing means the cat is angry.

20. Learn to speak cat. While even Attila the Hun probably enjoyed a bit of baby talk once in a while, cats have dignity and don't appreciate it. Never shout at your cat; if you must let her know she is doing wrong, try blowing a gentle puff of air in her face − that is what her mum would do. When your cat talks to you − a chirpy half-purr, half-mew, say − you must give a return sound, which your cat will take to mean, 'I hear you. I am responding.' I have had long conversations with some of the cats that have shared my life. If they hear you respond, they will invariably try something back, and on it goes.

21. Don't neglect your cat if you find a new lover, or have a baby. Some cats can tolerate your new love, especially if there are other cats in the home, but one change that is more than any cat can take is to find himself no longer allowed on the bed. Your cat believes it is his duty to guard you, the most cherished object of his love, from attack during your most vulnerable time. Sometimes, a neglected cat will be reduced to making a desperate cry for help. This can take the form of depositing urine or faeces about the home – even a neutered male may start spraying on furniture – and it's a clear signal from the cat that you are not listening. You must convince him that you still feel the same love for him you always did. Punishment has no place here. Introduce your new love, or baby, to your cat immediately, no matter how long this has been going on. Kitty needs to see that you are proud of him, so stroke and praise your cat in front of your new love. Never allow yourself or a friend to push your cat off the bed or couch. Work around your cat.

 Be vigilant. Any change in a cat's behaviour or mood merits a closer look. When you hear yourself say, 'Pussums doesn't usually do that', you could be noticing your cat is unwell. Repeat the following routine every day.

○ Run your hand from stem to stern, feeling for lumps and bumps and to see if your cat is sensitive to touch. Part the fur to check for fleas or hair loss.

○ Check your cat's eyes. Are they weepy? Does the skin of the inner lid cover part of the eye? In a healthy cat, it should be almost invisible.

○ Gently pull back the skin around the gums, and check the teeth are clean and the gums pink.

○ Sniff kitty's breath.

○ Sneak a peak under the tail (incorporate some serious rump scratching, so that kitty naturally raises her tail). Is everything clean and shipshape?

○ Squeeze each toe gently until the nails come out and you can check for breakages.

◯ Look and smell inside the ears. Do you see gunk, or black dots, which mean a mite infestation?

◯ Look at the coat. Is it shiny (or greasy, which is a sign of ill health)? If you take up a fold of skin on her back and let it go, does it spring right back where it belongs? If not, your cat is dehydrated. If the coat is dry, your cat would benefit from some fresh, steamed vegetables and a drop of olive oil. Comb every day to avoid hairballs.

 If your cat is old, make sure he has a cosy bed, away from draughts, that he can reach without mountaineering gear.

 Never give your cat cow's milk because most cats are lactose intolerant.

 Keep a check on your cat's weight. Many cats are overweight because commercial pet food is low in fibre, so your cat never feels full. Divide up her allotted daily intake into three soft meals, for morning, noon (if you are around) and night, and add some plain boiled rice for bulk. Don't be tempted to give her more. It's the extra little treats that do the real damage.

Rita, Roxanne, Jack, Eddie and Ginger

INGRID NEWKIRK
co-founder of the People for the Ethical Treatment of Animals,
Norfolk, Virginia, USA

The PETA office cats were all rescued from difficulties. Rita (far left) was living outside on a balcony in bitter winter. Roxanne (the black cat, top right) and Jack (grey tabby, top middle) were seized by police from a filthy trailer. Eddie and Ginger (the long-haired grey tabby and the long-haired orange tabby) were found in a junk car.

The cats supervise PETA's staff and perform special duties, including warming chairs, sorting papers, exercising editorial control by walking over computer keyboards, making absolutely certain that everyone knows exactly when it's lunch time, and alerting staff when a bird alights on the balcony. They are dearly loved.

Steven Appleby is an acclaimed cartoonist, whose work first appeared in *The New Musical Express*. Most famous for his cartoons in *The Guardian,* he lives in London.

Steven Berkoff is a writer, an actor (*A Clockwork Orange, Barry Lyndon*), and a director (*Coriolanus*). He speaks many languages, including Bengal cat. He lives in East London.

Amanda Bruns, her boyfriend, **Bradly Brown**, and their two cats live in Brooklyn, New York. Amanda is a well-known photographer, and has worked for magazines including *The Mail on Sunday*'s *YOU* and *Let Them Eat Cake*, and for the designer Marc Jacobs.

Grace Coddington is the flame-haired fashion director of American *Vogue*. Like Celia, she too started out as a very successful model in the Sixties, before joining British *Vogue* as a stylist. She is the author, with Didier Malige, of a book of her drawings called *The Catwalk Cats*. She lives in Manhattan.

Bethan Cole is the beauty editor of *The Sunday Times STYLE* magazine, and was formerly beauty editor of the relaunched *Nova* magazine, and thus has the softest skin in the world. She lives in the mean streets of Hackney.

Jilly Cooper is a best-selling author whose books have sold 11 million copies in the UK alone. Her latest novel, *Wicked!,*

was published in 2006. She lives in the Cotswolds, and uses an old-fashioned typewriter, submitting her copy with myriad crossings-out and addenda.

Jim Davis created the cartoon cat Garfield, whose life story appears in nearly three thousand newspapers worldwide, and whose life story has been made into two Hollywood movies (Garfield's life story, not Jim's), which proves being ginger doesn't necessarily hold you back.

Tracey Emin is one of the founder members of the Young British Artists movement, famous for her autobiographical works of art including *My Bed*, and *Everyone I Have Ever Slept With*. Tracey has donated two original works of art, both pictures of her beloved Docket, to be sold in aid of CHAT. She lives and works just off Brick Lane in East London.

Emma Forrest was one of the youngest writers ever to be hired by *The Sunday Times* as a columnist. She went on to write novels, and recently moved from Manhattan to Los Angeles, where she is currently working on screenplays.

Anais Gallagher is the daughter of Oasis-band-member Noel Gallagher and Meg Mathews. She lives with her mum, her Siamese cat Chewa and a black cat who was a stray, in Primrose Hill.

Ricky Gervais used to have big hair and sing in an Eighties pop band, but found success relatively late in life by creating

The Office and *Extras*. He lives in Bloomsbury with his girlfriend, the writer Jane Fallon, who takes second place to Ollie, a Tonkinese.

Celia Haddon writes a weekly advice column for pet owners in *The Daily Telegraph*, and has written many books on animals, including *Happy Bunny* and *100 Secret Thoughts Cats Have About Humans*.

Celia Hammond is a former *Vogue* cover model who established and runs The Celia Hammond Animal Trust. She lives between a room over one of her clinics in Canning Town, East London, and her home in East Sussex, near the Trust's sanctuary.

Judith Kerr is the children's author who created the best-selling series of Mog books, which finally ended with *Goodbye Mog*, in which the beloved tabby dies and comes back as a ghost. I, for one, have never quite recovered from the loss. Judith lives in Barnes, South-West London.

Sam Leith is a columnist and the literary editor of *The Daily Telegraph*. He is also the author of *Dead Pets*, a eulogy to all the animals he has loved and lost.

Deborah Moggach (what a catlike name) is an acclaimed novelist of titles including *Tulip Fever* and *These Foolish Things*. She recently adapted Jane Austen's *Pride and Prejudice* for the big screen.

Ingrid Newkirk is the co-founder of People for the Ethical Treatment of Animals, an organisation which, under Ingrid's leadership, has challenged the almighty McDonalds and KFC, and campaigned against the fur trade and factory farming.

Audrey Niffenegger is an artist who lives in Chicago. Her first novel, T*he Time Traveler's Wife*, became an international best-seller, and is currently being made into a film starring Brad Pitt.

Maggie O'Farrell is a novelist whose books include *After You'd Gone*, *My Lover's Lover* and *The Distance Between Us*. She lives in Edinburgh.

Catherine Tate, as well as not feeling strong enough to take on a disabled cat, is a comedian and writer whose *The Catherine Tate Sho*w has won both plaudits and viewers. She is also an actress, most recently appearing in the film *Starter for 10*, playing James McAvoy's mum, which is enough to depress anyone.

Lynne Truss is an author whose most recent books include *Eats, Shoots and Leaves*, the best-selling book about punctuation, and *Talk to the Hand*, a book about how rude people are nowadays.

Zoe Williams is a columnist and feature writer for *The Guardian*. Her menagerie of Spot and Summer is soon to be joined by a human baby. She lives in West London and drives a car that is so old she doesn't bother to lock it.

❧ ACKNOWLEDGMENTS ❧

With thanks to the indomitable Celia Hammond, without whom I would never have had the privilege of being the human companion to Susie and Sweetie. To Ingrid Newkirk, co-founder of People for the Ethical Treatment of Animals, who has saved so many animal lives, and reduced so much suffering. To Jane O'Shea and Clare Lattin of Quadrille, cat women both (Clare once demolished the chimney in her refurbished house to free a cat, which promptly scarpered, with barely a backwards glance). To Lawrence Morton, the designer, for his lateral thinking and patience, and for being able to differentiate between all the kitties. To Mary Davies, who edited the text within an inch of its life. To all the contributors to this book, who poured out their hearts and emailed me photographs of their own fur babies; in particular Tracey Emin, Grace Coddington and Judith Kerr, whose drawings were kindly donated to the cause, and auctioned to raise even more money. To Sotheby's London, who auctioned the drawings without taking a fee. To Lisa Herriott and Coline Henault, for helping to round up the famous people who agreed to contribute to this book. To Julie Burchill, who didn't want to be in the book but donated money anyway. To Robert Caskie, my agent, who waived his percentage, and he doesn't even own a cat! And, of course, to my very own fur babies, who have given me so much more than I can ever repay.

Credits

The publisher acknowledges the assistance of Jo Ireson and Joanne McGrath.

Illustration credits

The publisher apologises in advance for any unintentional omissions, and would be pleased to insert the appropriate acknowledgment in any subsequent edition.

Page 37 AlunCallender/www.aluncallender.com; page 55 © Michael Thomas/*Mail on Sunday*; pages 60 and 61 Grace Coddington; page 63 Bradly Brown; pages 73 and 75 Tracey Emin; pages 88 and 91 Alex Leith; page 96 Reproduced by permission of Geographers' A–Z Map Co. Ltd. © Crown Copyright 2007. All rights reserved. Licence number 100017302; page 98 © Judith Kerr; pages 102–3 © Steven Appleby.

Text credits

'Paddy and Buster' by Lynne Truss was first published in *The Mail on Sunday YOU* magazine on 4 March 2007.

'How to understand what your cat is saying' is extracted from *How to Read Your Cat's Mind: Purring Matters* by Celia Haddon, published by Little Books, London, in 2005.

'25 ways to make your cat adore you' is extracted and adapted with the author's permission from *250 Things You Can Do to Make Your Cat Adore You* by Ingrid Newkirk, published by Pocket Books, a imprint of Simon and Schuster, London (1997) and New York (1998).

For more information about The Celia Hammond Animal Trust
www.celiahammond.org
(01892) 783820/783367
Head office: High Street, Wadhurst,
East Sussex TN5 6AG
Registered Charity No. 293787

EMMA FORREST'S ALPHA CAT, PERRY

First published in 2007 by
Quadrille Publishing Limited
Alhambra House
27-31 Charing Cross Road
London WC2H OLS
www.quadrille.co.uk

This paperback edition published in 2008

EDITORIAL DIRECTOR: Jane O'Shea
DESIGNER: Lawrence Morton
EDITOR: Mary Davies
PRODUCTION: Vincent Smith, Bridget Fish

Cataloguing-in-Publication Data: a catalogue record
for this book is available from the British Library.

ISBN 978 1 84400 583 3

Printed in China